The Italian Presence
in Colonial Virginia

The Italian Presence in Colonial Virginia

Glenn Weaver

1988

Center for Migration Studies
New York

*The Center for Migration Studies is an educational,
non-profit institute founded in New York in 1964
to encourage and facilitate the study of socio-demographic,
economic, political, historical, legislative and pastoral
aspects of human migration and refugee movements.
The opinions expressed in this work are those of the author.*

The Italian Presence
in Colonial Virginia

First Edition
Copyright 1988 by
The Center for Migration Studies

CENTER FOR MIGRATION STUDIES
209 Flagg Place, Staten Island, New York 10304-1148

Library of Congress Cataloging-in-Publication Data

Weaver, Glenn.

The Italian Presence in Colonial Virginia.

Bibliography: p.
Includes index.

1. Italian Americans — Virginia — History.
2. Virginia — History — Colonial period, ca. 1600-1775.
I. Title.

F235.I8W43 1987 975.5'00451 86-32731

ISBN 0-934733-05-8

Printed in the United States of America

Acknowledgments

No work of historical scholarship would ever be completed, or even begun, without the assistance and encouragement of almost countless individuals. There are, of course, the usual family and friends, those who helped toss ideas about, and even those who would ask, almost daily, "How is it coming?" The names of such persons would fill several pages, but each, as he or she sees the final text, will doubtless recognize the part played in bringing together the final product.

Specific mention, however, must be made of several persons and institutions without whose direct moral and financial support there could have been no book. I am particularly indebted to Michael R. Campo, John J. McCook Professor of Modern Languages and Director of the Cesare Barbieri Center for Italian Studies at Trinity College; Borden W. Painter, Professor of History and former Dean of Trinity College; Andrew G. DeRocco, former Dean of Trinity College and presently President of Denison University; Dr. Peter Sammartino, Chancellor-President Emeritus of Fairleigh Dickinson University; the Reverend Lydio F. Tomasi, C.S. of the Center for Migration Studies; and Peter J. Knapp, Reference Librarian at Trinity College. All of these gave encouragement, counsel, and bibliographical and literary assistance. I also take this opportunity to thank Maggie Sullivan, my editor at the Center for Migration Studies, who also prepared the index, and Valerianne Pellito, who served as compositor to the text. Generous financial support was given by the several Trinity deans, the Trinity College Faculty Research Fund, the Cesare Barbieri Foundation of Trinity College, the National Italian American Foundation, and the Charles A. Dana Foundation, whose generosity allowed me to hold the Dana Research Professorship at Trinity College.

October, 1987
Hartford, Connecticut

Table of Contents

1

An English Way Station en Route to Virginia

Nicholas Pileggi, in *Esquire* Magazine for June, 1968, gave us what must unquestionably be the most outrageous title in all of American periodical literature: "How We Italians Discovered America and Kept it Clean and Pure While Giving it a Lot of Singers, Judges, and Other Swell People".[1]

While Mr. Pileggi was writing with his tongue extending far into his cheek, the title, nonetheless, reminds us of two important facts of Italian American historiography. First, Italian American historians have been fully aware, and understandably proud, of the Italian contribution to American life. Second, Italian American historians have been more concerned with the "Singers-and-Judges" period than they have been with the years between Columbus and the great Italian influx which began in the 1880s.

General surveys of the Italian experience in America, therefore, tap lightly on the pre-Revolutionary period, merely noting the presence of several well-known individuals of Italian origin as isolated cases of people who attained either fame or notoriety almost by accident. In none of the broad treatments is there any indication that Italians were to be found in any sizeable numbers.

Perhaps the older understanding of early Italian immigration to British North America and the United States during its formative years was best expressed shortly before the outbreak of the American Civil War, by Eliot Lord, Special Agent for the Tenth Census of the United States. Lord wrote that "from the earliest days of the colonization of North America up to less than a generation ago, the influx from Italy was barely a trickle, so inconsiderable that a microscope is almost needed to distinguish the Italian resident population in 1850".[2]

For his own generation, Lord's observation was eminently correct, but, had he been familiar with the history of pre-Revolutionary Virginia, he would have known that from the beginning of that colony's settlement, and indeed in the very creation of the Virginia Company in 1606, there was an "Italian presence" which, to continue Lord's metaphor, never approached a torrent, but was at least a "constant" in that colony's history. This text examines this "presence" and seeks to make an evaluation as to its historical significance.

---

[1] Nicholas Pileggi, *Esquire*, 69 (June, 1968), 69 ff.

[2] Quoted in Emilio Goggio, "The Dawn of Italian Culture in America", *The Romanic Review*, X (July-September, 1919), 250n.

However, the Italian "presence" in colonial Virginia is more easily appreciated when it is understood that there was also something of an Italian "presence" in England long before the Europeans' discovery of America. Virtually from the time of Augustine of Canterbury (A.D. 597), Italians had made their way to England as clergymen, traders, seamen, bankers, and courtiers. By the reign of Henry III (1216-1272), Italian merchants were selling Mediterranean and Oriental goods at shops in English cities and at the fairs which were held in almost every English market town. Italian bankers were lending money to both monarchs and nobles, collecting Papal tithes and transporting them to Rome, and developing a system of bills of credit which would ultimately make England the most important commercial nation in the world. London was England's center of Italian banking and trade, and by the time of Edward III (1327-1377), and especially as the Jews had been expelled from the realm in 1290, Lombards and Florentines (particularly the house of Bardi and Peruzzi) operated large banking establishments in Lombard Street.[3]

From about 1317, Venetians dominated the foreign trade of England, with Venetian vessels bringing to the island kingdom all sorts of goods which had been gathered in Venice. By the end of the fifteenth century, Italian artisans, including glass blowers and silk weavers, took up residence in various parts of England. Most of these people changed their religion to Anglican, and some of them took on English variants (spellings) of their family names. Italian mercenaries, both footsoldiers and sailors, were frequently recruited from Venice and Sicily, and often these men, after their term of service had expired, chose to remain in England. There were also those who "jumped ship" to remain in London or Bristol, rather than return to their home base of Genoa or Venice, especially as the trading importance of these ports declined in the fifteenth and sixteenth centuries.[4]

The Italian cultural influence upon England was of tremendous importance, and the Italian inspiration of English writers from Chaucer to Milton is so familiar that it need not be rehearsed here. Italian medicine, too, was highly regarded in England, as is evidenced by the fact that virtually all court physicians from the time of Henry VIII on were Italian. Perhaps the most famous of the Elizabethan court physicians was Dr. Cesare Aldemare, a Venetian, whose fee for a single professional attendance and consultation was £100! Aldemare's son, Julius Caesar Aldemare, dropped the family name, choosing to be known simply as Julius Caesar. Julius was educated at Oxford and Paris, holding doctorates in both civil and canon law. During the reigns of Elizabeth and

[3] Giovanni Ermenigildo Schiavo, *The Italians in America Before the Civil War* (New York and Chicago: Vigo Press, 1934), Pp. 14-15.

[4] *Ibid.,* Pp. 14-18; K.R. Andrews, "English Voyages to the Caribbean, 1596-1604: An Annotated List", *William and Mary Quarterly,* 3rd Series, XXXI (April, 1974), 243-254. After 1353, Venetian and Genoese carriers dominated England's trade with the Mediterranean. D.M. Palliser, *The Age of Elizabeth: England under the later Tudors: 1547-1603* (London and New York: Longman, 1983), Pp. 281, 289.

James I he held numerous court offices, and in 1603 he was knighted by the latter. In 1614 he was appointed Master of the Rolls, and it was in this and earlier capacities that he had much to do with the creation of the Virginia Company of 1606 and its re-organization in 1609.[5]

Italians also had what almost amounted to a monopoly on positions in the royal musical establishment, and there were, in fact, families, or even dynasties, of court musicians such as the Lupo, Ferrabosco, Taliaferro, Memmo, Draghi, Albricci, Leneare, and Corbetta clans. The Lupos alone, beginning with Ambrosio Lupo, who in 1559 became one of Elizabeth's court musicians, had at least nine members in the royal employ. These court musicians seem to have been well-paid, and sometimes they became men of property. Nicholas Leneare, whose descendants came to Virginia in the 1660s, became Master of the Music under James I in 1603 at a pension (or salary) of £220 a year. Nicholas and several other members of his family held extensive property in London, East Greenwich, and Blackheath.[6]

The list of distinguished "Englishmen of Italian extraction", as Giovanni E. Schiavo calls them, goes on and on. Before his death in 1608, Aberico Gentili, born near Pisa in 1552, was one of England's most illustrious jurists and writers on legal subjects.[7] Giovanni Florio (1553?-1625), friend of William Shakespeare, Ben Jonson, Richard Hakluyt, and the Earl of Southampton, was of Tuscan origin, his parents being Waldensians who had taken refuge in England. The elder Florio was pastor of the Italian Protestant congregation in London, and it was he who wrote the first Italian-English dictionary, plus several treatises on grammar and rhetoric. Florio, Senior, was also tutor in French and Italian to Prince Henry, son of James I.[8] The younger Florio had some small part in the "expansion of England", when as early as 1580, Hakluyt had him translate "Cartier's Voyages to Canada" into English for inclusion in Hakluyt's famous collection of narratives of exploration and discovery.[9]

Certainly not to be forgotten is Sir Horatio Pallavicino (d. 1600), a member of a celebrated Italian family, the elder branch of which ruled the Po River district of Stato Pallavicino and the cadet branch of Genoa which was noted for its historians and cardinals. Horatio was Collector of the Papal taxes in England during the reign of Queen Mary, but upon the death of Mary and the accession of Elizabeth, Pallavicino abjured his Romanism, refused to return to Italy, kept the monies he had collected during the past five years, lent the same to Queen

---

[5] G.E. Schiavo, *The Italians in America Before the Civil War*, Pp. 19-20; Article, "Sir Julius Caesar", *Encyclopaedia Britannica*, Eleventh Ed.

[6] Article, "Thomas Lupo", *Dictionary of National Biography* (hereafter cited as *DNB*), XII, 284-285; G.E. Schiavo, *Italian-American History*, 2 vols. (New York: The Vigo Press, 1947-1949), I, 25n.; Reginald M. Glencross, editorial note to Will of Elinor Laniere, *Virginia Magazine of History and Biography* XXVII (October, 1920), 341n. (Hereafter cited as *VMHB*).

[7] *The Italians in America Before the Civil War*, p. 129.

[8] *DNB*, VII, 1003-1006.   [9] *Encyclopaedia Britannica.* 11th Ed.

Elizabeth at a usurious rate, and made, thereby, one of the largest personal fortunes in England. Horatio was naturalized in 1586 and knighted in 1587.[10]

Sir Horatio Pallavicino's widow, a year and a day after her husband's death, married Sir Oliver Cromwell, the great-uncle of Oliver Cromwell, Lord Protector during the English Civil War. Two of Sir Horatio's sons, Henry and Toby, married, in 1606, Sir Oliver Cromwell's two daughters of a previous marriage. Sir Horatio's daughter, Baptina, married Henry Cromwell, Sir Oliver's eldest son and heir. Sir Horatio's eldest son, Edward, born of his first wife, "a very mean person" from the Low Countries, was, in deference to the wishes of Sir Horatio's second wife, declared illegitimate and disinherited.[11] Whatever the internal embarrassments of the Pallavicino family may have been, both Toby and Edward seem to have been friends by the time of the creation of the Virginia Company, in which both were investors. Edward was also a member of the Council of the London Branch of the Company.[12]

Also among the small shareholders in the Virginia Company was Clinton Vivion (or Vivian), several of whose descendants went to Virginia early in the eighteenth century. If the Vivion family tradition has any historical validity, the Vivions were the most remotedly-established English family of Italian extraction, being descended from a Roman officer of that name during the reign of the Emperor Nero, with the first "English" Vivion having come to England with the Roman conquerors.[13]

Many of the Italians who went to England during Elizabethan and early Stuart times were members of the upper and middle classes — physicians, merchants, artists, musicians, and teachers — and these have been easy enough to trace.[14] There were, however, almost countless others who enjoyed fame in neither the old country nor the new. Some of these "small people" can be identified by the naturalization records, as in each case of naturalization, the country of origin is indicated clearly. "Origins" are also given in the numerous extant records of membership in London gilds and the French and Italian Congregations of that city.[15] G.E. Schiavo has extracted a random list of such individuals, and it is significant to note that few of them could be otherwise identified as Italian:

[10] A.L. Rouse, *The Elizabethans and America* (New York: Harper and Row, 1959), p. 43.

[11] Article, "Sir Horatio Pallavicino", *DNB*, XV, 97-98.   [12] *Ibid.*, 97.

[13] Alexander Brown, *The First Republic in America* (Boston and New York: Houghton Mifflin and Co., 1898), Pp. 361, 554, 590, 383; Susan Myra Kingsbury, ed., *The Records of the Virginia Company of London*, 4 vols. (Washington: Government Printing Office for Library of Congress, 1906-1935), III, 605, *et passim. Cf.* List of Stockholders in the London Company, *Virginia Magazine of History and Biography*, IV (January, 1898), 303-304.

[14] Charles Brunk Heineman, "Vivion Family of Virginia", *VMHB*, XLVI (October, 1938), 352.

[15] E.G. Kirk and Ernest F. Kirk, *Returns of Aliens Dwelling in the City and Suburbs of London from the Reign of Henry VIII to that of James I*, 4 Vols. (Aberdeen: for the Huguenot Society of London, 1900-1908, being vol. X of the *Publications* of the Huguenot Society of London), *passim.*

Jasper de Gattye

Baltesar Santes

John Grey

John Gillam

Francis Moliganzer

Giles Corner

Innocent Commy

Peter Frangilder

John Delegge

John Regalln

Katheren Osmastrach

Anthony Counties

Godfrey Sokes

Peter Foxe

Jacob Romcom

James Moore

Zakary Mounty

Baptiste Fortune

James Maryan

Gabriell Brangier

Gaspyn Sonhall, Physician

Raphaell Gettye

Anthony Brusquett

Franceses Syneball

Ambrose Lux

Joseph Luxe

Frances Kennythe

Yppolite Santyne

Cosyno Graffie

James Flotrye

Nicholas Degotes

Stephan John

Dyno Pickering

Jacob Frauncis

Aserbo Vilutell

Epolito Lyamount

Askano Lyamount

Shepion Vilutell

Bastian Rise

Lyon Sampson

Vincent Goodgerden

Christopher De Mount

Dare Polis

Incenot

Frances Pytcher

John Portinary

Francisco Benson

Peter Cottye

John Baptist

Peter Fanall

Thomas Cannot

Domynick Bowshett

Gasperin Gaffin[16]

When it is remembered that the English Renaissance coincided with the reign of the Tudor monarchs, it is easy to see why England, depending culturally upon Italy and the Low Countries, would have had a fascination with Italy and why the policy on naturalization would have been quite liberal. Newcomers of special

[16] Giovanni Ermenegildo Schiavo, *Italian-American History*, 2 vols. (New York: The Vigo Press, 1947-1949), I, 13-16.

talent (or wealth) could be made "denizens", a status which allowed them to reside in England and to hold property. Naturalization was by special act of Parliament or by royal letter, and this gave the individual the full rights and privileges of Englishmen. As both of these procedures involved considerable financial outlay, many foreigners — Italians included — lived in England with neither property nor civil rights.[17]

The Italian newcomers to England were especially welcomed as the arbiters of culture. Well placed Englishmen were, at the same time, eager to visit Italy to see for themselves how the civilized life was lived.[18] Italian books on etiquette had long been popular in England, and just at about the time of the settlement of Jamestown, Englishmen were learning from the Italians the art of eating with a table fork. In 1611, one Crozat published a small book, *Crudities, Hastily Gobbled up in Five Months' Travel in France, Savoy, Italy, Etc.*, in which he described carefully the correct Italian method, presumably then unknown in England, of conveying food from the table to the mouth.[19]

The Italian influence was not universally praised. A anonymous author, writing about 1612, in what was obviously a tract for the times, quoted Roger Ascham, a Cambridge scholar of the previous century, sharply censuring —

> those English, Italianate travelers: [insisting that] For Religion, they get Papistrie or worse; for learning, lesse commonly than they carried out; for Policies, a factious heart, a mind to meddle in all new matters; for experience, plenty of new mischiefs never known in England before; for manners, varieties of vanities, and change of filthy living. [But even those who remain at home, he noted, could not fail to be corrupted] by precepts of fond bookes of late translated out of Italian into English [and] sold in every shop in London.[20]

The English fascination with Italy was not exactly a one-way street, for several well-known Italians found much to admire in England, oddly enough, especially

---

[17] Richard Conant Harper, *The Course of the Melting Pot Idea to 1910* (New York: Arno Press, 1980), p. 38.

[18] Nicholas Farrar, who became a member of the Virginia Company in 1619, had traveled and studied for a year in Germany, Spain, and Italy. "Farrar Genealogy", *VHMB*, VII, (April, 1900), 435. The Farrar family, despite the claim of several Italian-American historians, was not Italian and was in no way related to the Italian family of Ferraro. John Parry, Secretary to Sir George Yeardly, acting Governor of Virginia (1616-1617) and Governor (1626-1627), had twice passed through Italy. *VHMB*, XLIX (January, 1941), 55.

[19] Article signed, "Soladis", *The Virginia Historical Register*, II (July, 1849), 156. D.M. Palliser, in *The Age of Elizabeth: England under the later Tudors 1547-1603* (London and New York: Longman, 1983), p. 8, notes that most Elizabethan courtiers, and the Queen, could both speak and read the Italian language, and that there were, during the late sixteenth century, several Italians who were well-known tutors who instructed English sophisticates.

[20] *The New Life of Virginia...Being the Second Part of Nova Britannia* (London: Felix Kyngston, 1612), in Peter Force, *Tracts and Other Papers Relating Principally to the Origin, Settlement and Progress of the Colonies in North America*, 4 vols. (Washington, D.C.: Peter Force, 1836-1846), I, 21-22.

the English Church. Paolo Sarpi, the famous Venetian theologian, historian, scientist, and legal scholar, was greatly attracted to the Anglican Book of Common Prayer and, during his ongoing controversies with Popes Clement VIII and Paul V, he gave serious thought to taking refuge in England.[21] Sarpi's *History of the Council of Trent* was completed in 1606 and published in England in 1619, several years before the Italian edition appeared. Englishmen, from James I on down, believed that Sarpi's vehement anti-Papal stance was to be interpreted as demonstrating the author's belief that the Church of England, rather than that of Rome, was the true Catholic Church.[22]

Even more convinced than was Sarpi of the superiority of the Church of England was Marco Antonio De Dominis, Archbishop of Spoleto, who in 1616 actually defected to Anglicanism and went to England, where, in an impressive ceremony in St. Paul's Cathedral, he was welcomed by the King and Archbishops into the English Church. After serving as rector of a small parish in rural Berkshire, De Dominis had second thoughts. In 1621 he returned to Rome, only to become the target of the Inquisition and to die in prison in 1624.[23]

By the time of the first planting of Virginia in 1607, Italians — whether coming directly from Italy or of Italian descent — were certainly not novelties in England, and of no small significance was the fact that they were to be found at every level of English society. In the following chapters, various methods were employed in this tedious, and treacherous, sifting to determine the "Italian presence" in colonial Virginia. Extensive use was made of passenger lists for ships sailing for the colony, land records, court records, registers of indentured servants, tax lists, and handbooks on family names.[24] Attention was paid to seeking out obviously Italian names, but this is one of the least reliable tools, as some names which may "look" Italian (alternating vowels and consonants with a final vowel) may not be Italian at all, or, indeed, may not even represent another Mediterranean name.

Among such names turning up in early Virginia are Rosse, which in some cases is a variant of Ross and not a variant of Rossi; and Farlo, which is a variant of Farley. The Jerdone family was from Scotland,[25] Duppa was an old Herefordshire family,[26] and Bolito (Bolithoe) is English.[27] Combe is English,

---

[21] "Paolo Sarpi", *Encyclopaedia Britannica*, 11th Ed.

[22] Edward A. Gosselin and Laurence S. Lerner, "Galileo and the Long Shadow of Bruno", *Archives Internationales D'Historie des Sciences*, 25 (December, 1975), 233.

[23] "Marco Antonio De Dominis", *Encyclopaedia Britannica*, 11th Ed.

[24] Among the most useful of these handbooks is Elsdon C. Smith, *New Dictionary of American Family Names* (New York: Harper & Row, 1973). Hereafter cited as *Names*.

[25] Bishop [William] Meade, in *Old Churches, Ministers, and Families of Virginia*, 2 vols. (Philadelphia: J.B. Lippicot & Co., 1917), I, 468, gave, incorrectly, the origin of the Fuqua family as French. *See also,* W.G. Stanard, *Some Emigrants to Virginia* 2nd ed. (Baltimore: Southern Book Company, 1953), p.48.

[26] John Burke, *Encyclopedia of Heraldry* (London: Henry G. Boher, MDCCCXLIV), unpaged.

[27] James P.C. Southall, "Further Notes Concerning the Cocke Family of England", *William and Mary Quarterly*, Second Series, X (April, 1930), 154.

Curle is Scottish, and Bobo (and all its variants) is Polish.[28] Nimmo was a common name in Britain,[29] and Paramore (Parramore and other variants) has been traced in England to at least A.D. 1273.[30] Ferrar or Farrar, which has sometimes been identified as being related to the Italian family of Ferrara,[31] seems to have had no Italian connection at all, being, instead, an old Yorkshire family related to Robert Ferrar, Bishop of St. David's, who was burned at the stake during the Marian persecutions.[32] Farsi seems Italian enough, but this name turns out to be a variant of the French name, Forsee or Farci.[33]

One would be tempted to identify Anthony Longo and John Francisco as Italian. Both, however, were free blacks living in Virginia in the middle of the seventeenth century, as perhaps were Silvedo and Manuel Rodrequez and John Pedro, and Bashaw Ferdinando.[34]

One of the most vexing problems in identifying surnames of Italian origin is with names ending in "gni". Although this ending is common in Italian names, it is also a Gaelic genetive, meaning "son of". Hence, Broccagni is Scottish meaning "son of Brocan", and so it is with Colmagni (son of Colman), Gottagni, Scilagni, Mailogni, and Tolagni.[35]

Another methodological difficulty is that of making identification through the female line. Males can be traced, even with, as we shall see, changes in spelling of the family name. Women of the time surrendered their family names at time of marriage, and the line of descent can thus be easily lost. Allowing for the fact that many more males bearing Italian names came to Virginia than females, even as loosely as we are defining "Italian" here, the "Italian presence" may have been even greater than the available data would indicate.

And finally, in this regard, there is the fact that spellings of the most common English family name often varied from document to document, or within a

[28] E.C. Smith, Names, 47, 92, 103.   [29] WMQ, First Series, V (October, 1896), 135.

[30] Charles Waering Bardsley, A Dictionary of English and Welsh Surnames, (London: Henry Frowde, 1961), p. 353.

[31] G.E. Schiavo, The Italians in America Before the Civil War, p. 129.

[32] Virginia Magazine of History and Biography, III (April, 1896), 359n. Editorial note (presumably by Philip A. Bruce) to Decisions of Virginia General Court, 1626-1628, from Robinson Transcripts, Virginia Historical Society Manuscript Collection.

[33] Cameron Allen, "Isaac Lefebvre (Lefevre) of Manakin Town and his Immediate Descendants", VMHB, 74 (January, 1966), 32.

[34] Edmund S. Morgan, Review of County Court Records of Accomack-Northampton, Virginia by Susie M. Ames (Charlotteville: University of Virginia Press for Virginia Historical Society, 1973) in VMHB, 82 (April, 1974), p. 393; List of Tithables-Northampton County, Virginia, 1666, VMHB, X (January, 1902), 259; Philip Alexander Bruce, Social Life of Virginia in the Seventeenth Century (Williamstown, Massachusetts: Corner House Publishers, reprint of 1968), p. 261; T.H. Breen and Stephen Innes, "Myne Owne Ground": Race and Freedom on Virginia's Eastern Shore, 1640-1676 (New York: Oxford University Press, 1980), pp. 69, 81-83, 103-111.

[35] George F. Black, The Surnames of Scotland: Their Origins, Meaning and History (New York: New York Public Library, 1946), Passim.

single document. Such a common Virginia name as Randolph was, for example, sometimes rendered as Randall or Randle; Percy was Persy, Piersey, or Pierse; Bland was written sometimes as Blund or Blunt; Goggin sometimes came to the second page of a single document as Colkin, Cockin, Cockeyn, Cocyn, Cokain, Gackin, Gakin, Gookins, or Gooking. James C. Southall, writing at the end of the nineteenth century on the Cocke Family, declared that in the Virginia records "the spelling...is lawless beyond our imagination".[36] With such being the case with familiar English names, the reader may well wonder what the seventeenth-century keeper of records might have done with a totally foreign name which he may never have seen in print nor ever before heard pronounced.

[36] James C. Southall, *VMHB*, III (January, 1896), 289.

2

Three Virginia Gentlemen of Italian Extraction

When on April 10, 1606, King James I issued the charter for the Virginia Company, there was little doubt that all who had participated in the venture had done so in the twofold hope of establishing an English beach head on the North American continent and deriving a profit for themselves as investors. This economic intent was made abundantly clear in the charter provision that all trade in the settlement would be the monopoly of the Virginia Company for the first five years, and, since it was what was then known as a "regulated" company, the profits would be divided proportionately among individual investors at the end of that time. The commercial nature of the "Company" became even more obivous at the time of its reorganization in 1609 as a joint-stock company, when 659 individuals, a majority of them merchants, and fifty-six London "companies" — the vestiges of the late Medieval guilds — "bought into" the enterprise at £12 10s. per share with the expectation of turning their modest investments into huge fortunes.

And, given the commercial nature of the Virginia enterprise, all persons who came to the colony during its earlier years were technically employees of the company. Given the then-dominant English economic theory of Mercantilism, those sent to the colony by the company should have been men possessed of such occupational skills as would lessen England's dependence upon other countries for such products as wine, olive oil, silk, tar, turpentine, and glassware.[37]

Among the 105 men and boys who in 1607 began the settlement of Jamestown were four carpenters, a blacksmith, a barber, a tailor, two bricklayers, a mason, a surgeon, and twelve common laborers[38] — certainly what might have been an adequate contingent to set up and maintain a small English outpost in the wilds of North America. With the arrival in early 1608 of the First Supply (i.e., the second detachment of men sent to the colony), came two refiners (presumably of gold), two goldsmiths, and a jeweler — obviously in expectation of finding gold in or near the settlment.[39] The most obviously mercantilist basis of selection

---

[37] Mercantilism, reduced to its simplest terms, meant: 1) import nothing that can be produced at home, and 2) always have the value of exports exceed that of imports.

[38] Philip L. Barbour, ed., *The Jamestown Voyages Under the First Charter, 1606-1609*, 2 vols. (Cambridge: University Press, 1969), II, 383.

[39] *Ibid.*, II, 398.

of settlers for Virginia was the inclusion in the Second Supply, which arrived in the fall of 1608, of several "Dutchmen" (or Germans) and Poles, men supposedly skilled in the production of tar, pitch, potash, and glass.[40]

Of the Dutchmen we know little — little more than their first names: Adam, Francis, and Samuel.[41] Of the Poles we know even less, although Captain John Smith immortalized them in his account of how they once saved his life by frightening off the Indians and thus preventing the Captain's capture.[42] At any rate, Germans and Poles were "exotics" among the earliest settlers at Jamestown; Italians probably were not.

Nevertheless, Italian American historians have hoped to find Englishmen of Italian extraction among the earliest arrivals, and it was through a clerk's calligraphic error that the first seemingly Italian name appears in the record. In the first list of those who arrived in Virginia on the *Discovery, Godspeed*, and *Susan Constant* was one Edward Brinto, stone mason.[43] Several pages later the same individual's name is spelled Brinton, and so it is in the two additional references to this person — the first spelling being an obvious deletion of the final letter of the name. The spellings have invariably been reproduced in various editions of the early account.[44] If there were indeed an Italian presence among the initial Jamestown settlers, the name or names are unknown. All that can be said here is that of the 105 men and boys, the names of only 66 have been recorded.[45]

With the arrival of the "First Supply", however, we meet our first individual who may be said with certainty to have represented the "presence". On October 7, 1607, Captain Christopher Newport sailed from London on the *John and Francis* with a cargo of supplies and 120 passengers. Among those who landed at Jamestown on January 2, 1608, was Edward Gargana, listed among the 29 "gentlemen" who made the voyage. Of Gargana's background we know little, other than that his name was Italian[46] and that, given his honorific title, he was a person of considerable status in England. Conway Whittle Sams has suggested that all of those listed as "gentlemen" were members of good families who had seen military service in the recent war with Spain and that, having been discharged from the English forces in the Netherlands, were being sent to Virginia to provide for the defense of the settlement.[47] Captain John Smith, to

---

[40] *Ibid.*, II, 418-420.   [41] *Ibid.*, I, xxviii.   [42] *Ibid.*, II, 442.   [43] *Ibid.*, I, 383.

[44] *C.f.* Lyon Gardiner Tyler, ed., "Proceedings of the English Colonies", in *Narratives of Early Virginia, 1606-1625* (New York: Charles Scribner's Sons, 1930), Pp. 120, 162, 169, 170.

[45] Barbour (*The Jamestown Voyages*, I, xxviii) notes that of the 295 persons who arrived in Virginia before October 1, 1608, the names of only 239 (80% of the total) are known.

[46] Meaning "dweller at the sign of the frog;...[or] with the characteristics of a frog". E.C. Smith, *American Family Names*, p. 172. Philip Alexander Bruce wrote that Gargana was "probably either of Italian or Portuguese blood". *Social Life of Virginia in the Seventeenth Century* (Williamstown, Massachusetts: Corner House Publishers, reprint of 1968), p. 261.

[47] Conway Whittle Sams, *The Conquest of Virginia: The Second Attempt* (Norfolk, Va.: Keyser-Doherty Printing Corporation, 1929), p. 816.

whom we owe the basic listing of early new arrivals in the colony, has been criticized for being "somewhat indiscriminate" in his application of the term, one scholar even going so far as to say that Smith applied the term "gentleman" to all of his companions except enlisted soldiers and common laborers.[48] Nevertheless, the fact that Gargana was a person of quality is evidenced in the fact that in each mention in the records he is identified as "Mr." Gargana.

Gargana's first efforts on behalf of the Virginia Company was to help organize Argall's Town (or Argall's Gift), one of several "plantations" set up as agricultural/trading communities. Evidently his work was highly regarded, for when in 1616 the company began to parcel out landholdings to individuals, Gargana received a tract of 400 acres. When the Virginia House of Burgesses first convened in 1619, he was sent to Jamestown to represent Argall's Town. When it was discovered that Gargana's land grant fell within the tract already assigned to the Governor, his claim was transferred to Henrico.[49]

Gargana's wife Ann and daughter Adria did not come to Virginia until 1611. Both Edward and Ann Gargana died in 1619, and the Gargana lands were inherited by their daughter Adria who had, meanwhile, married Captain Thomas Harris, a shareholder in the Virginia Company who had come to the colony in 1611 on the *Prosperous*. The Harrises had several children, and their progeny was large; probably the best-known of them was the twentieth century popular historian and novelist, James Branch Cabell. Adria made at least one return trip to England (1621), perhaps to place her children or step-children in an English school. The Harris lands, known later as "Longfield", ultimately became part of the large plantation known as "Curles".[50] Although Edward Gargana left no male descendants, others bearing the name, with many variants, came to the colony later.[51]

In 1618, the Virginia Company, in an effort to increase the population of the colony at no cost to the Company, introduced the "head-right" system, whereby any person who came to the colony at his own expense or paid the passage for another person would receive a grant of fifty acres of land. Included in the provision were members of one's family, indentured servants (*i.e.*, servants under contract to serve from four to seven years in exchange for passage), and, later, slaves and convicts. Over the years, large landholdings were built up in the

---

[48] Francis Burton Harrison, "Footnotes on Some XVII Century Virginians", *VMHB*, LI (April, 1943), 162.

[49] Virginia State Land Office, County Abstacts, Henrico County, Virginia State Library; Lyon Gardiner Tyler, *The Cradle of the Republic* (Richmond: The Heritage Press, 1906), Pp. 22, 232; Annie Lash Jester, *Adventurers of Purse and Person* (Princeton: Princeton University Press, 1956), Pp. 202-203; Mrs. Henry Lowell Cook, "Maids for Wives", *VMHB*, LI (January, 1943), 77.

[50] Mrs. H.L. Cook, "Maids for Wives", p. 72; A.L. Jester, *Adventurers*, Pp. 7, 203; L.G. Tyler, *The Cradle of the Republic*, p. 222.

[51] The name, incidentally, as applied to this person was one of many variations in the early records, appearing as Gargana, Garganna, Gurgunye, Gurgahny, and Virgany.

colony, as individuals with financial capital purchased the head rights of others, whether they were ship captains, single individuals, or simply relatives. As a landholding of fifty acres was rather insignificant in a country where land was a plentiful commodity, head-right certificates came to pass as money until they fell into the hands of someone who would have a sufficient number of head-rights to present to the colony surveyor to mark out a substantial holding.

On March 6, 1636, Richard Cocke, a neighbor of Thomas Harris, patented 3,000 acres for bringing to the colony "3 score persons", among whom was Elizabeth Gargaine.[52] Three years later Ellis Gargame was one of forty persons brought to Virginia by Cocke.[53] These two were probably related to Mrs. Harris. Others bearing variants of the name were Nicholas Garigrine (1648)[54], Samuel Garingoe (1652)[55], and Francis Gargen (1653)[56]. In 1757, one John Baptista Gurgonna was sent to the colonies as a convict, the record simply stating that he was sent on the *Thetis*, with the destination not given.[57]

In 1610, another "gentleman" of Italian extraction, Albiano Lupo, arrived in Virginia on the *Swan*. It is uncertain as to exactly why Lupo came to the colony. Lupo was then 26 years of age and married to Elizabeth, then a girl of but 13 years. Elizabeth did not go to Virginia until 1616, when she arrived on The *George*. A daughter, Temperence, was born in 1617.[58]

When the Virginia Company charter of 1609 brought in individual merchants and English liveried companies as shareholders, several of the "companies" and individual investors sent representatives to Virginia to look after their particular interests. Often these "representatives" were members of the family or relatives of prominent individuals within the liveried company.[59] Albiano Lupo was of the London musical family, and the Musicians Company was an investor under the charter of 1609. Also, his father, Philip Lupo, Sr., a London goldsmith, was a member of the Goldsmith's Company,[60] although not himself a personal investor.

---

[52] Spellings here and following are as they appear in the record. Nell Marion Nugent, *Cavaliers and Pioneers, Abstracts of Virginia Land Patents and Grants, 1623-1800*, 3 vols. (Richmond: Dietz Press and Virginia State Library, 1934-1959), I, 54.   [53] *Ibid.*, I, 120.

[54] George Cabell Greer, *Early Virginia Immigrants* (Baltimore: Genealogical Publishing Co., 1960), p. 123.

[55] N.M. Nugent, *Cavaliers and Pioneers*, I, 268.   [56] G.C. Greer, *Early Virginia Immigrants*, p. 123.

[57] Peter Wilson Coldham, *English Convicts in Colonial America*, 2 vols. (New Orleans: Polyanthos, 1974-1975), I, 109.

[58] John Camden Hotten, *The Original Lists of Persons of Quality: Emigrants; Religious Exiles; Political Rebels; Serving Men Sold for a Term of Years; Apprentices; Children Stolen; Maidens Pressed; and others who went from Great Britain to the American Plantations: 1600-1700*, 2nd ed. (New York: J.W. Bouton, 1880), p. 245.

[59] Alexander Brown, *The Genesis of the United States*, 2 vols. (Boston: Houghton Mifflin Co., 1890), I, 228; II, 542, 550.

[60] Albiano was the younger brother of Philip Lupo who came to Virginia in 1621. Hotten, *Lists*; W.G.

At the time of Albiano Lupo's arrival in Virginia, Governor Thomas Lord De La Ware decided to erect two small forts on opposite sides of what is now Hampton Creek in the present city of Hampton.[61] Lupo was a member of the earliest group to enlist or "be enlisted" for service at De La Ware's forts. Evidently he was either placed in charge of one of the forts or had similar military responsibilities, for almost immediately he acquired the title of "Lieu-tenant", by which he was known for the remainder of his life.[62]

Lord De La Ware's forts were never of any real military importance, and, indeed, the question may arise as to whether these small defenses near the mouth of the James River were ever actually completed. Nevertheless, it was here that the settlement which took its name from the previous Indian village of Kickotan (the simplest form of at least a score of different spellings) began. A new status was given to the settlement in 1618, when on November 18, the Company divided the Colony of Virginia into four "boroughs" or "corporations" — Jamestown, Charles City, Henrico, and Kickotan, which was later renamed Elizabeth City. At this same time, all those having arrived in the colony before that date with the intention of becoming permanent residents were declared "Ancient Planters". Both Albiano and Elizabeth Lupo (as well as Edward and Ann Gargana) were so designated.[63]

Albiano Lupo was an enterprising man, and soon he was bringing "servants" to the colony at his own expense. In 1617, John Slaughter, John Hayes and Hester Wheeler came in the *George*. Elizabeth Hayden came in the *London Merchant* in 1620. Daniel Palmer and Jacob Herin came in the *Warwick* in 1621. Henry Draper came in the *George* in the same year. Also one Joseph Ham, a young man in his teens, came at about this time. In 1621, Philip Lupo, Albiano's elder brother by two years, also came in the *George*, and for several years he made his home with Albiano and Elizabeth. A William Lupo also lived in Elizabeth City for some time before 1622.[64]

By what must have been regarded as a somewhat unusual procedure, Albiano Lupo was able to take double advantage of transporting servants. On

Stanard, *Some Emigrants to Virginia*, 2nd ed. (Richmond: The Bell Book and Stationary Company, 1916), p. 55.

[61] Ivor Nöel Hume, *Here Lies Virginia: An Archaeologist's View of Colonial Life and History* (New York: Knopf, 1963), 49.

[62] This was doubtless a strictly military title, as the county office of Lieutenant did not appear before the creation of counties in 1634. The law of that year ordered "Lieutenants to be appointed the same as in England, and in a more especial manner to take care of the war against the Indians...". William Walter Hening, *The Statutes at Large; Being a Collection of all the Laws of Virginia from the First Session of the Legislature in the Year 1619*, 13 vols. (Charlotteville: University of Virginia Press, Facsimile Reprint of 1969), I, 224.

[63] S.M. Kingsbury, *Records of the Virginia Company*, I, 373.

[64] Hotten, *Lists*, Pp. 245, 248; N.M. Nugent, *Cavaliers and Pioneers*, I, 5; Caroline Kemper Bulkley, "Notes on Immigrant Lawsons of Tidewater", *WMQ*, 2nd series (October, 1933), 243; W.G. Stanard, comp., "Abstracts of Virginia Land Patents", *VMHB* (October, 1893), I, 194-195.

March 18, 1620, he was admitted to the Virginia Company "for 1 share and for three more men more which he sent 1 1/2 shares [for a total of] 2 1/2 shares".[65] Lupo was also able to take advantage of the head right, and although he sold at least one such right,[66] he put in a claim for 350 acres. The claim was granted by Governor Sir Francis Wyatt on September 1, 1624. Elizabeth, in what must have been something of a *coup* for the time, received 50 acres in her own right.[67] The Lupo's 400 acres placed them among the largest of the 35 earliest landholders in Elizabeth City, their tract being exceeded only by that of Captain Roughly Croslaw's 500 acres.[68] The two Lupo holdings, incidentally, were separated by a small stream later known as Lupo's Creek.[69]

The infamous Indian raid of 1622 brought tragedy to the Lupos of Elizabeth City. William Lupo was killed during the raid,[70] and Temperence, who would then have been a girl of five years, may also have been a victim, as her name does not appear in the records after that date.

Even before the Indian massacre, the fortunes of Albiano Lupo were on the wane. Early in 1622, the governor, strongly suspecting an Indian raid, reorganized the colony's system of defense. Captain William Tucker was placed in command of the entire region on the north shore of the James,[71] thus superseding Albiano Lupo in whatever local military authority he may have previously enjoyed. Also, in 1624, the Virginia Assembly created the office of Commander, one to be appointed for each settlement, and whose duty it would be to see that each family had sufficient firearms and ammunition to prevent further destruction by the Indians. Albiano Lupo was not given such a commission, nor was he commissioned as lieutenant to the commander, an office for which the act also provided.[72] Actually, it was William Tucker who was given the title of Commander for Elizabeth City and Thomas Purefoy who was made lieutenant.[73]

Albiano Lupo died in 1626, and his will was probated at James City on October 9 of that year. Witnesses to the document were Thomas Spillman and John Slaughter,[74] one of Lupo's former servants. Elizabeth Lupo died shortly

[65] S.M. Kingsbury, *Records of the Virginia Company*, III, 60, *C.f.* List of Shareholders in London ⁻ Company, *VMHB*, IV (January, 1897), 303, for discrepancy in date.

[66] W.G. Stanard, "Abstracts of Virginia Land Patents", p.195.

[67] Land Office Catalog, Elizabeth City County, Virginia State Library; W.G. Stanard, "Abstracts", Pp. 194-915.

[68] Hotten, *Lists*, p. 273; "A List of Tithes and Landowners in Virginia, 1625", *VMHB*, XVI (July, 1908), 14, and editor's note p. 8; Alexander Brown, *The First Republic in America* (Boston and New York: Houghton Mifflin and Co., 1898), 623.

[69] N.M. Nugent, *Cavaliers and Pioneers*, I, 5.   [70] Hotten, *Lists*, p. 193.

[71] S.M. Kingsbury, *Records of the Virginia Company*, III, 623, 664-665.

[72] Philip Alexander Bruce, *Institutional History of Virginia in the Seventeenth Century*, 2 vols. (New York: E.P. Putnam's Sons, 1910), II, 15, 33.

[73] Minutes of Council and General Court, 1622-1624, *VMHB*, XIX (April, 1911), 121n., 122n.

[74] *Ibid.*, p. 119.

thereafter, and the Lupo landholding was divided. John Chandler purchased a large portion of the tract, and later fifty acres were purchased to form part of the large plantation known as "Celeys". The entire tract would ultimately become part of the city of Newport.[75]

Meanwhile, Philip Lupo had moved across the James to Warwick's Squack (or Warrasquoake), one of the company settlements in what would become Isle of Wight County. Philip Lupo may have shared in the estate of Albiano, and in his will of 1670 Philip identified himself as the son and heir of Philip Lupo, goldsmith of London,[76] but never did Philip enjoy the status of Albiano during his earlier years in Virginia. Never was Philip identified in the records as "gentleman", and never was the title of "Mr." applied.

The only other Lupo to come to the colony was another William, who in 1643 was one of the forty persons brought, presumably as an indentured servant, by Sir Francis Wyatt.[77] This William seems to have disappeared early, and it was Philip's numerous descendants (with the names of Philip and James turning up in each generation) who became numerous in Isle of Wight and Surry Counties. The Lupos did not become great landholders in the Isle of Wight, although they were probably what may have been called "lesser gentry". In the land census of 1704, for example, James Lupo appears on the list, with 45 acres in Isle of Wight County. Of the 252 Isle of Wight landholdings, which varied downward from Samuel and William Bridger's 12,900 and James Samson's 12,000 acres, James Lupo's 45 acres stood with John Branch's 45 acres at the bottom of the list.[78]

Although the Isle of Wight Lupos did not acquire great landed property, they were a respected clan, several of whom married into such landed families as Branch, Willison, Bridges, Bidgood, Brantley, Correll, Almond, and Atkinson.[79] And although the Isle of Wight members of the Lupo family themselves left small personal estates,[80] for several generations Lupos appeared regularly in

[75] W.T. Stauffer, "The Old Farms Out of Which the City of Newport was Erected with Some Account of the Families which Dwelt Therein", *WMQ*, 2nd series, XV (July, 1935), 251; N.M. Nugent, *Cavaliers and Pioneers*, I, 156.

[76] John Bennett Boddie, *Seventeenth Century Isle of Wight County, Virginia* (Chicago: Chicago Law Publishing Co., 1938), p. 232; Blanche Adams Chapman, *Wills and Administrations of Isle of Wight County, Virginia, 1647-1800*, 3 vols. (n.p., 1938), I, 14.

[77] N.M. Nugent, *Cavliers and Pioneers*, I, 148.

[78] Rent Rolls of Virginia, 1704-1705, in Thomas Jefferson Wertenbaker, *The Planters of Colonial Virginia* (Princeton: Princeton University Press, 1922), Pp. 183-247. *See, VMHB*, XXIV (July, 1921), 338, for a slightly different listing.

[79] Blanche Adams Chapman, *Wills and Administrations of Isle of Wight County, Virginia*, p. 31; Blanche Adams Chapman, ed., *Isle of Wight County Marriages* (n.p., 1933), Pp. 4-5, 79, 97; Blanche Adams Chapman, *Marriages of Isle of Wight County, Virginia, 1628-1800* (Baltimore: Genealogical Publishing Co., Inc., 1976), p. 4; J.B. Boddie, *Seventeenth Century Isle of Wight*, p. 232.

[80] Clinton Torrence, comp., *Virginia Wills and Administrations: 1632-1800, an Index* (Richmond: The William Byrd Press, [n.d.]), Pp. 267-268; Will of Patience Cary of Isle of Wight County, in *Edward Pleasants*

the court records in the trusted and respected capacity of appraisers of estates and executors of wills.[81]

Of all the Italian names to appear in early Virginia, that of Lupo was one of the slowest to undergo change, and some of the earlier corruptions may simply reflect the phonetic spelling of a clerk who had never seen the name in written form. Although one branch of the family retained the spelling of "Lupo" until the American Revolution,[82] "Lupoo", "Lupoe", "Lumpo", and even "Lingo" became common variants. As late as the 1980s, Isle of Wight County members of this family spelled the name as "Looper". The Lingo branch of the family became landholders in Accomack County on the Eastern Shore, with James Lingo firmly established in the "planter" class holding 200 acres and William Lingo holding 300 in 1704.[83]

Still a third gentleman of Italian extraction to arrive in early Virginia was John Polentine who probably came in the fall of 1608 in the "Second Supply".[84] Polentine's wife Rachell and daughter Margaret did not come until several years later. Polentine was a leading figure in the Company settlement at Henrico, and in 1619 he represented that borough in the House of Burgesses.[85] Shortly before or after the massacre of 1622, Polentine moved to Warrasquoake, and for several sessions he was a Burgess from that community.[86] In 1624, he served as clerk of the court for Basse's Choice in what would become Isle of Wight County. He had also acquired a military (militia) status, as in that year he was identified as Captain John Polington.[87]

Polentine, like most other early Virginians of status, began to bring in servants and acquire land. Among those killed on Polentine lands in the 1622 massacre was one identified simply as "Symon, an Italian",[88] but there must have been

---

Valentine Papers, 4 vols. (Richmond: The Valentine Museum, [n.d.]), I. 300-301; Blanche Adams Chapman, *Wills and Administrations of Isle of Wight County*, I, 66-68, 74; II, 27, 39, 56; III, 53, 86.

[81] *Ibid.*, I, 66-68; II, 27, 39, 56; III, 53.

[82] Philip Lupo was commissioned Ensign on November 6, 1777. Notes from the Isle of Wight County Records, *VMHB*, XI (July, 1903), 85.

[83] *Edward Pleasants Valentine Papers*, I, 301; Isle of Wight County Records, *WMQ*, 1st series, VII (April, 1899), 250, 275, 307; Blanche Adams Chapman, *Marriages of Isle of Wight County*, p. 85. In the Accomack County probate records are the wills of William Lingo (1750), Littleton Lingo (1771), Caleb Lingo (1789), and John Lingo (1792). *Virginia Wills and Administrations, 1632-1800*, p. 261; Ralph T. Whitelaw, *Virginia's Eastern Shore: A History of Northampton and Accomack Counties*, 2 vols. (Gloucester, Massachusetts: Peter Smith, 1968), II, 763; Thomas Jefferson Wertenbaker, *The Planters of Colonial Virginia* (Princeton: Princeton University Press, 1922). p. 241.

[84] G.E. Schiavo, *The Italians of America Before the Civil War*, p. 129; Lyon G. Tyler, *Encyclopedia of Virginia Biography*, 5 vols. (New York: Lewis Historical Publishing Company, 1915), I, 306.

[85] H.R. McIlwaine, ed., *Journals of the House of Burgesses of Virginia, 1619-1658/9* (Richmond: [n.p.], 1940), Pp. vii, 3.

[86] *Ibid.*, Pp. viii, 22, 26, 29, 42.

[87] J.B. Boddie, *Seventeenth Century Isle of Wight County, Virginia*, p. 703.   [88] Hotten, *Lists*, p. 193.

many others, as in 1626 Polentine was listed as holding 1,600 acres of land.[89]

In 1624, as the affairs of the Virginia Company were in such a poor financial state that it had become obvious that the Crown would void the charter, Polentine was sent by the Virginia Assembly to present to the English authorities the cause of the settlers themselves.[90]

Although his efforts on behalf of the colonists and the Company were ineffectual, Polentine made the most of his journey to England, organizing a partnership with John Preen and Thomas Willoughby to engage in trade between London and Virginia. Several vessels — the *Peter and John, Samuel,* and *Endeaveror* — were employed in the business, but the partnership ended with Polentine's death in 1628.[91]

Polentine may have died in England or at sea, and the settlement of his estate presented great difficulty for his widow. The executors seem to have been somewhat less than honest, and from the extant probate records it would seem that the executors benefited more than the widow.[92] The will of John Polentine no longer exists, but there seem to have been still other legal and financial complications involving partners and relatives.

The tracing of Polentine kin presents unusual difficulty, as the family name has undergone almost unbelievable change. Even during John's lifetime the name appeared in the Journals of the House of Burgesses as Polentine (1619), Pollington and Powntie (1624), and Pollingtone (1623).[93] Margaret was the only known child, but there could have been other relatives in England or in the colony. Certainly others bearing the name did come to Virginia. In 1643, a John Pollentine was one of sixteen persons brought to Isle of Wight County by Lt. Col. Arthur Smith,[94] and in 1674 Nicholas Polentine was among 14 persons brought to New Kent County.[95] Given the certain variations, one might wonder whether the Nicholas Gillintine who patented land in King William County in 1714,[96] the Nicholas Giloline who patented land in New Kent County in the same year,[97] or the John Gillintine who patented land in Bedford County in 1767[98] might not be members of the Polentine clan.

[89] J.B. Boddie, *Seventeenth Century Isle of Wight County, Virginia,* p. 31n. *See also, VMHB,* XVI (July, 1908), 13.

[90] G.E. Schiavo, *The Italians in America Before the Civil War,* p. 129.

[91] Minutes of the Council and General Court, 1622-1629, *VMHB,* XXX (October, 1922), 356; *VMHB,* XVI (July, 1908), 31-34; W.W. Henry, "The First Legislative Assembly in America — Sitting at Jamestown, Virginia", *VMHB,* II, (July, 1894), 90; Conway Whittle Sams, *The Conquest of Virginia: The Third Attempt, 1610-1624* (New York: G.P. Putnam's Sons, 1939), p. 446.

[92] Minutes of the Council and General Court, 1622-1629, *VMHB,* XXX (October, 1922), 356.

[93] *Journal of the House of Burgesses of Virginia, 1619-1658/9,* Pp. vii, viii, 22, 26, 29, 42.

[94] N.M. Nugent, *Cavaliers and Pioneers,* II, 198. The will of John Bollentine was probated in Norfolk County in 1761. *Virginia Wills and Abstracts, 1632-1800,* p. 41. A John Pollentine is listed as a Norfolk County landholder in 1711. N.M. Nugent, *Cavaliers and Pioneers,* III, 116.

[95] *Ibid.,* II, 142.   [96] Land Office Catalog, Virginia State Library.

[97] N.M. Nugent, *Cavaliers and Pioneers,* III, 154.   [98] Land Office Catalog, Virginia State Library.

3

A Spy, Some Servants, and Six Glassblowers

Before the revocation of Virginia's charter in 1624, Italians, either directly from Italy or English persons of Italian extraction, had come to the colony in considerable numbers. Some stayed but briefly, many died early, but those who remained and survived were absorbed into the colony's basic ethnic stock.

One whose stay was short was that individual identified simply as "a gentleman from Venice". He appeared in 1613, apparently a convert from Roman Catholicism seeking refuge. Soon, however, he reverted to his Romish faith and began to proselytize. As the laws (and charter) of the colony permitted no religion other than the Church of England, and as it was soon determined that he was a Spanish spy, the "gentleman" was sent to England and ultimately on to Spain.[99]

Others were most welcome. John and Susan Virgo (Vigo) came to Virginia sometime between 1609 and 1615 on one of the several voyages of the *Treasurer*. Until at least 1624, they were servants in the employ of Captain William Pierce of Mulberry Island.[100] William Benge came in 1619 in the *Marigold*.[101] Elias Legardo, assumed by one writer to have been a Sephardic Jew,[102] came in 1621 in the *Abigail*. Legardo was thirty-eight years of age at the time of his arrival, somewhat old for an indentured servant. At the time of the massacre he was living with the family of Anthony Bonoll, although not listed as a servant.[103]

In 1622, one "Mr. Punte", apparently in the employ of Henry Spelman, began trading English goods and provisions from a small pinnace up and down the James River. When the Governor mounted a retaliatory expedition against

[99] Alexander Brown, *The First Republic in America* (Boston and New York: Houghton Mifflin and Co., 1898), Pp. 175, 189.

[100] *Ibid.*, p. 613; Annie Lash Jester, *Adventurers of Purse and Person, Virginia, 1607-1625* (Princeton: Princeton University Press, 1956), p. 45; John Camden Hotten, *The Original Lists of Persons of Quality; Emigrants; Religious Exiles; Political Rebels; Serving Men Held for a Term of Years...*, 2nd ed. (New York: J.W. Bouton, 1880), p. 240.

[101] Carl Boyer, III, *Ship Passenger Lists: The South, 1558-1825* (Newhall, Calif: Pub. by the Compiler, 1979), p. 54.

[102] Michael Tepper, *New World Immigrants: A Consolidation of Ship Passenger Lists and Associated Data*, 2 vols. (Baltimore: Genealogical Publishing Co. Inc., 1979), I, 16.

[103] Hotten, *Lists*, p. 261; Jester, *Adventurers*, p. 65.

the Indians following the massacre, Punte's pinnace was requisitioned to carry supplies for the colony troops.[104]

As nearly one-third of the entire population of Virginia had been killed in the massacre, the Company ordered the governor to take a census of the living and to make a complete listing of the dead. In this head-counting, one of the most precise and complete ever taken, a surprising number of Italian names appear. Among the dead were William Lupo at Elizabeth City, "Symon an Italian" at Warrasquoake, Daniel Viero (who came in the *George* in 1623) at Shirley Hundred, and William Perigo at Henrico Island.[105]

Living persons with obviously Italian names listed in the census were Stephen Callo (who came in the *George* in 1624), servant to Edward Waters at Elizabeth City, John Pergo and Anthony Bruni "on the River" at James City, and William Vintine or Vincene (who, at age 39, came in the *Mary and James*) and Joane Vincene, his wife, both at Henrico. Rebecca Rosse and two children were reported as living at Shirley Hundred.[106]

Not all of those who had survived the great massacre had hopes for a new and better day. On March, 28, 1625, as the Minutes of the Council and General Court recorded, John Verone, a "servant boy" to Hugh Crowther, "did hange himself with an Irone dogg chaine" in the loft of Crowther's house.[107]

By the time of the great massacre, even the Virginia Company itself was in danger of falling apart. No fortunes had been made by the shareholders, and none of the Company's original objectives had been achieved. Neither gold nor silver had been found, nor was there a Northwest Passage to the Indies. Tobacco had, indeed, become a marketable commodity, but even here none of the profits, small as they may have been, were returned to the Company itself. Actually, such limited success as had been achieved was the work of numerous "sub-companies" which had set up such settlements as Kickotan, Warrasquoake, Smith's Hundred, Martin's Hundred, Martin's Brandon, and about forty others.

Trade with the Indians had never been developed, largely, it was thought, because the English had nothing to offer the Indians in exchange for furs and corn. The glass works which had been set up by the Dutchman in 1608 had been a total failure,[108] but the idea was revived in June, 1621, when Captain

---

[104] George Sandys to John Ferrar, April 8, 1623, from Newport Newes, *VMHB*, VI (January, 1899), 242; Governor and Council of Virginia to the Virginia Company, James City, January 30, 1623/4, *VMHB*, VI (April, 1899), 375.

[105] Hotten, *Lists*, p. 172; William Clayton Torrence, "Henrico County, Virginia: Beginnings of Its Families", *WMQ*, 1st series, XXIV (October, 1915), 125; Kingsbury, *Records of the Virginia Company*, III, 565. Jester, *Adventurers*, p. 14.

[106] Hotten, *Lists*, Pp. 171, 172, 202; Carl Boyer, III, *Ship Passenger Lists*, Pp. 26, 28, 30, 57, 60; W.C. Torrence, "Henrico County, Virginia...", *WMQ* 1st series, XXIII (October, 1915), 124, 128; Jester, *Adventurers*, p. 58. "Rosse" may have been "Rose".

[107] *VMHB*, XXIII (January, 1915), 8.

[108] Philip Alexander Bruce, *Economic History of Virginia in the Seventeenth Century*, 2 vols. (New York:

William Norton presented the Virginia Company with a plan to create a sub-company for the production of beads and other glass items. Norton proposed that six Venetian glassblowers and their families be sent. The proposal was accepted quickly, and a "company" was created to carry out the operation. Norton and his family and servants would go to Virginia at Norton's expense, and the glassblowers and their families would be sent at the cost of the investors. The glassblowers would contract for seven years of service and would share in all profits from the operation.[109]

Norton had little trouble in recruiting his glassblowers (or perhaps he had already made his contacts before the plan had been accepted), and by mid-summer the six Italians and their families[110] set sail on the *Marmaduke* as part of a passenger list of 80 persons which included several "brides" and several young English gentlemen.[111]

Upon their arrival in Jamestown, the Italians were lodged temporarily in the "guesthouse" (or inn) which had been built by Lieutenant Whitaker,[112] although Pierce Bernardo, one of the men, and his family lived for a time with Captain Norton.[113] The glassworks and the accompanying living quarters were set up on the mainland about a mile outside the Jamestown palisade.[114]

From the beginning, it seemed that a curse had been placed upon the project. Before the main structure had been completed, it was blown down by a windstorm and had to be rebuilt.[115] Also, what was described as a "general sickness" spread through the population. The Italians were totally incapacitated for several weeks and, most importantly, Captain Norton died.[116]

Direction of the operation was taken over immediately by George Sandys who had arrived in Virginia as "local treasurer" in October, 1621. Sandys was in many ways suited to the management of the glassworks and to the revitalization of the entire settlement. Sandys was the son of the Archbishop of York and a

---

The McMillan Company, 1895), II, 440-441; Charles E. Hatch, Jr., "Glassmaking in Virginia, 1607-1625", *WMQ*, 2nd series, XXI (April, 1941), 126.

[109] S.M. Kingsbury, *Records of the Virginia Company*, I, 484, 493, 499.

[110] There is some question as to the size of the Venetians' party. The *Records of the Virginia Company* (I, 500-1) says 6 Italians and their families and four Italians, two wives and their children (I, 513). A twentieth-century writer says that there were 16 Italians in all. Henry Chandler Forman, "The Bygone 'Subberbs' of James Citie", *WMQ*, 2nd series, XX (October, 1940), 479. Wesley Frank Craven, *Dissolution of the Virginia Company: The Failure of a Colonial Experiment* (New York: Oxford University Press, 1932), p. 191, says that there were six men and their families, or eleven people in all.

[111] Alexander Brown, *The First Republic*, Pp. 454-455.

[112] Instructions to Governor Sir Francis Wyatt, July 24, 1621, Heming, *Statutes*, I, 116; Kingsbury, *Records of the Virginia Company*, III, 477.

[113] Charles E. Hatch, Jr., "Glassmaking in Virginia", p. 136.

[114] Kingsbury, *Records of the Virginia Company*, III, 494, 640.   [115] *Ibid.,* IV, 23.

[116] Alexander Brown, *The First Republic*, p. 505.

brother of Sir Edwin Sandys, Treasurer of the Virginia Company since 1619, and one who had spent time in Venice during the 1590s. Unfortunately for Sandys' hopes, however, the Indian massacre of 1622 virtually precluded extensive trade with the Virginia Indians, and this defeated the glassworks' chief purpose. Although neither Jamestown nor the glassworks was attacked, the massacre was a least a contributory factor in the glassworks' ultimate failure, as the English investors used the occasion to refuse any further significant financial support for the project.[117]

Nevertheless, Sandys determined to make the glassworks a success, whether the investors would or not. As Sandys was interested in industrial production in general, he attempted to follow the example of the several governors of Virginia in applying the Statute of Artificers of 1563, an act of Parliament which required laborers to work from 5 a.m. to 7 or 8 p.m. from mid-March to mid-September, and from daybreak to sunset for the remainder of the year. The English "gentlemen" in the colony had already set a bad example, for none of them had ever before performed manual labor, and none was about to begin to perform manual labor in Virginia. Even the common laborers who had come to the colony were unwilling to conform, coming to work late in the morning and leaving the job whenever they became fatigued. Furthermore, Negro slavery had already been introduced, and there was an understandable identification of manual labor with involuntary servitude.[118] Thus, it was hardly to be expected that the highly-skilled Venetian glassblowers would have taken kindly to an insistence upon what must have amounted to a fourteen-hour, summertime work day.

Indeed, one must wonder how these men had been induced to participate in the arrangement at all. From Venice to Virginia was a long jump geographically, but culturally the distance was even greater, and from the very beginning of the glassworks project there had been dissatisfaction on the part of the Venetians — a dissatisfaction which had taken the form of foot-dragging, procrastination, and outright prevarication.

First, the sand needed for glass production could not, according to the Venetians, be found in Virginia, and Sandys had to send to England for the proper kind. Next, the fires of the furnace could not be sustained because of a presumed flaw in its construction. Finally, in an act of desperation, one which the Venetians assumed would guarantee their return to Europe, Vincentio, the foreman, totally destroyed the furnace when he "crakt it with a crow of iron". Although the destruction of the furnace might have been passed off as an

[117] W.F. Craven, *Dissolution of the Virginia Company*, p. 294; H.C. Forman, "The Bygone 'Subberbs'", p. 479; Lyon Gardiner Tyler, ed., *Narrative of Early Virginia, 1606-1625* (New York: Charles Scribner's Sons, 1930).

[118] Edmund S. Morgan, "The Labor Problems at Jamestown, 1607-1618", *American Historical Review*, LXXVI (June, 1971), 600-610.

accident, Vincentio's wife, the victim of a recent beating by her spouse, told the whole story to Sandys.[119]

Sandys, belatedly realizing that the Venetians would never put the plant into operation, lost his temper completely, declaring of them that "a more damned crew hell never vomited".[120] It took little convincing on Sandys' part that there was little future for a glassworks that had never even produced a single bead,[121] and on June 15, 1625, the Virginia Council, on behalf of the glassworks sub-company, ordered that Vincentio and Bernardo "shall have their passe to goe for Englande [,] they entering a thousand pownds bond to ye Adventurers [investors] of the glasse works to serve the remainder of ye tyme of theire Covenants, if they [the investors] shall require it [,] either in England...or to serve the time out in Virginia...".[122]

On whether Vincentio and Bernardo, or any of the others, ever returned to Venice, or even to England, the record is silent. In the winter of 1623-1624, the census listed as living at the glass house: Vincentio, Bernardo, "ould Sheppard his son" (whoever that may have been), Richard Tarboorer, Mrs. Bernardo, one Boniventuro, and presumably the Bernardo child.[123] It is to be noted that there is no Mrs. Vincentio and that there are listed only three or four adult males. In 1625, the Bernardos and their child were living at "the Treasurer's Plant", meaning of course, the home of George Sandys.[124]

The end of the glassworks coincided with the end of the Virginia Company, and the failure of the glassworks might rightly be regarded as the ultimate failure in a long series. On May 24, 1624, King James I, partly at the request of the officers and investors of the Virginia Company, revoked the charter, and Virginia thus became a royal colony. On July 15, 1624, King James appointed "commissioners for Virginia to receive the charter, seals, and letters of the Virginia Company, and [to] attend to the affairs of the colony". On the "commission" were two of our old friends, Englishmen of Italian extraction, Edward Pallavicino and Sir Julius Caesar.[125]

---

[119] Kingsbury, *Records of the Virginia Company*, IV, 23-24.   [120] *Ibid.*, IV, 23-24.

[121] Ivor Noël Hume, Chief Archaeologist for Colonial Williamsburg, says that extensive archaeological investigations of the glasshouse site conducted between 1931 and 1950 have uncovered the entire plant showing a complete, typical, seventeenth-century glassworks, but that despite the most careful examination of the debris and overlaying soil, not a single bead or fragment of glass goblet has been found — conclusive evidence that the glassworks never produced a single, saleable piece of glass. *Here Lies Virginia: An Archaeologist's View of Colonial Life and History* (New York: Alfred A. Knopf, 1963). Pp. 198-199.

[122] *Minutes of the Council and General Court of Colonial Virginia*. H.R. McIlvaine, ed., second ed., (Richmond: Virginia State Library, 1979), p. 56. *C.f.* Kingsbury, *Records of the Virginia Company*, IV, 565.

[123] Hotten, *Lists*, p. 172.

[124] Charles E. Hatch, Jr., "Glassmaking in Virginia, 1607-1625", *WMQ*, second series, XXI (July, 1941), 227.

[125] Edward D. Neill, *Virginia Carolorum* (Albany, N.Y.: Joel Murrill's Sons, 1886), Pp. 11n. ff., 13.

4

Virginia-Italian Subjects of the Crown

Virginia's transition from charter colony to royal colony was made altogether without incident. Although the governor would, under the new system, be appointed by the crown, the representative House of Burgesses would remain the same and, with the creation of counties in 1634, representation therein would be by county, rather than by borough, hundred, or plantation. All grants of land made by the Virginia Company were confirmed immediately by the royal governor, and new grants would be made according to the old head-right system. Tobacco would remain the colony's principal export and, much to the economic detriment of the plantations, corn would fall to a minor crop. Although royal governors would lament what was to become a one-crop economy, the crown, and all in authority in England, would urge stepped-up production of the noxious weed.

Virginia tobacco growers of Italian extraction might have noticed that in October of 1626, the new king, Charles I, had appointed Philip Burlamachi, Henry Lee, Thomas Brownest, and William Archwell, all London merchants, as royal agents in the importation of tobacco. Burlamachi, who for several years would be the largest importer of Virginia tobacco in all of Europe, was born in Sedan, France, of Italian parents, and was, at the time of the tobacco arrangement, a naturalized English citizen.[126]

Some of the Italians in the colony had done quite well for themselves — those of higher social status, that is. Others had not fared quite so well, and, at least one — young John Verone — had decided that Virginia held no promise at all for him.[127] When it is remembered that of the 7,289 individuals who came to Virginia during the first 30 years of the colony, 6,040 of them had died, or put another way, that no fewer than five out of every six persons had succumbed to disease,[128] the survivors should have been happy just to be alive.

---

[126] Alfred Rice, "A Brief History of Regulation and Taxation of Tobacco in England", *WMQ*, second series, IX (April, 1929), 73, 75; Neville Williams, "England's Tobacco Trade in the Reign of Charles I", *VMHB*, 65 (October, 1957), 408-409.

[127] *See above.*

[128] Alexander Brown, *The First Republic in America* (Boston and New York: Houghton Mifflin and Co., 1898), Pp. 285, 329, 612; Philip Alexander Bruce, *Social Life of Virginia in the Seventeenth Century* (Williamstown, Massachusetts: Corner House, reprint of 1968), p. 16.

By 1625, John and Susan Virgo had worked out the term of years called for in their contract. Although their names do not appear in the land records, they seem to have acquired some personal property and were expected to assume a place of responsibility within the community. On March 5, 1628, however, John Virgo was, at a session of the Council and General Court held at Jamestown, one of several persons charged with refusing to assist the Provost Marshall in "setting an unruly fellowe in the stockes", and for this obstinacy he was fined 40 pounds of tobacco and ordered to post £40 sterling to appear before the court on March 8. Virgo failed to appear on the scheduled date and thus forfeited his £40.[129] There is no further mention of John Virgo in the colony records.

William and Joane Vincene (as the name appears in the earliest record) seem to have had similar troubles. Although the Vincenes were not servants and were listed in the census of 1624 as living in a separate household or muster (and here the name is given as Vintene),[130] and although William was to be identified in the records as a "planter", they were obviously persons of lowly station, and Joane, to put it mildly, was also something of a scold.

On November 25, 1624, Joane was charged by Mrs. Alice Boyse (and note the "Mrs.") with slander in Joane's declaring that Mrs. Boyse "hath had a Bastard". Joane was sentenced to make apology while standing in a white sheet. This, however, Joane refused to do, and the General Court took the easy way out and dismissed the case.[131] On March 6, 1625, Joane (here spelled Vincent) was again in court, this time for slandering Richard Taylor, a man of considerable importance who had represented Henrico in the House of Burgesses, with the charge that Taylor had had sexual relations with seven of the thirteen women living in the community.[132]

Twelve days later, William, too, made his appearance in court in a case, the exact nature of which cannot be figured out from the extant records, involving Thomas Harris and John Chambers. At any rate, Vincent (as the name appears here) failed to appear and was ordered to pay Harris and Chambers 30 pounds of tobacco each.[133] A repeat performance in court came on July 7, 1626, when William (along with two others) charged that the same Harris had appropriated land to which he had no legal claim.[134] Harris, it will be remembered, was the husband of Adria Gargana.

Others by the name of Vincent appear in the early Virginia records, although

---

[129] *Minutes of the Council and General Court of Colonial Virginia*, H.R. McIlwaine, ed., second ed. (Richmond: Virginia State Library, 1979), Pp. 190, 196.

[130] John Camden Hotten, *The Original Lists of Persons...who went from Great Britain to the American Plantations, 1600-1700*, 2nd ed. (New York: J.W. Bouton, 1880), p. 202.

[131] *Minutes of the Council and General Court of Colonial Virginia*, p. 31.

[132] *Ibid.,* p. 96; Minutes of the Council and General Court, *VMHB*, XXV (July, 1917), 227. This printing of the "Minutes" has footnote identification of persons involved in the case.

[133] *Minutes of the Council and General Court of Colonial Virginia*, p. 97.   [134] *Ibid.,* p.129.

they may have been no relation to William and Joane Vincent. On July 13, 1635, one Thomas Vincent patented 100 acres in Elizabeth City County,[135] and in April, 1671, a George Vincent patented land in Stafford County.[136]

Both the new form of government and the old agricultural system assumed the continued use of indentured servants, and persons under contract arrived in Virginia in a steady stream. During the first seven years of royal control, it seems that no persons of Italian extraction came to the colony. In 1633, however, Thomas Crompe patented 500 acres in James City County for bringing in nine persons, including one whose name appears variously as Lewis De Poma, Depoma, Depona, Dipina, and Di Pino.[137]

The steady Italian stream began in 1635, and from that point on, arrivals of persons of Italian extraction can be traced through the land records, as the exact name of each person for whom a head-right was claimed had to be recorded. Furthermore, the location of the patented land is invariably a part of the record, but this listing may have had little to do with where those who were "transported" entered into service. Nor is the date of the land patent necessarily the time of arrival of the person listed for the head-right, as patents were usually given months, and sometimes years, after the arrival.[138]

Nevertheless, on the basis of available data, in 1635, Leonard Leonardo was brought to Virginia by Robert Herbert of Accomack County on Virginia's Eastern Shore[139] and James Cameo was brought in by Thomas Johnson, Junior, of Northampton County, also on the Eastern Shore.[140] The English records show that in that same year Marie Lerrigo, age 19, and Anthony Stilgo (or Stilyo), age 21, were certified in London by both civil and ecclesiastical authorities as to their conformity to the doctrines of the Church of England and thus were allowed to go to Virginia — Lerrigo on the *Safety* and Stilgo on the *Assurance*.[141] There is no record, however, of their having reached the colony.

But, one might well wonder what the origin of all this concern for Anglican conformity was? William Laud had become Archbishop of Canterbury in 1633, and it was his intention to keep Protestant dissenters out of the colonies, preferring to keep them at home, where his policy of "Thorough" would enforce both doctrinal and liturgical conformity. On the other hand, Gregorio

---

[135] Virginia State Land Office, County Abstracts, Elizabeth City County, Virginia State Library.

[136] *Minutes of the Council and General Court of Colonial Virginia*, p. 246.

[137] Abstracts of Original Land Patents, prepared by W.G. Stanard, *VMHB*, IV (July, 1896), 75; Nell Marion Nugent, *Cavaliers and Pioneers*, 3 vols. (Richmond: Dietz Press and Virginia State Library, 1934-1959), I, 31-32; George Cabell Greer, *Early Virginia Immigrants, 1623-1666* (Baltimore: Genealogical Publishing Co., 1960). p. 94.

[138] Avery E. Kolb, "Early Passengers to Virginia: When Did They Really Arrive?", *VMHB*, 88 (October, 1980), 401ff.

[139] G.C. Greer, *Early Virginia Immigrants*, p. 203.   [140] *Ibid.*, p. 58.

[141] Hotten, *Lists*, Pp. 111, 123, 571.

Panzani, the charismatic Papal Legate, was creating a great stir in London and was making converts to the Roman faith daily.[142]

In 1636, John Rocto[143] and Gabriel Adeo[144] were listed in headrights for Charles City County, Leon Boloe for Henrico County,[145] and Burston Christo for Elizabeth City County.[146] George Lento was one of 14 persons brought by Henry Southell for 400 acres "upon the Chesopeian Shore within the territorie of Lynhaven",[147] the name then given the coast of Chesapeake Bay between Cape Henry on the coast and Hampton Roads at the mouth of the James. This region would later become Princess Anne County.

Also in 1636, John Veale was one of seven persons brought to the colony for headrights "on the south side of the Nansemond River",[148] a location on the south bank of the James River, some 20 miles upstream from Lynhaven Bay, and what would later become Nansemond County. Members of the Veale family lived in the lower James region throughout its colonial period. In 1761, George and Thomas Veale took the oath of conformity to the doctrines of the Church of England as vestrymen of Portsmouth Parish,[149] and in 1768, Thomas Veale represented Norfolk in the Virginia Assembly.[150]

Robert and Elizabeth Pistole represented two of the 30 headrights of John Neale for 1,500 acres of Accomack County, patented on June 18, 1636.[151] A probable descendant, Charles Pistole, in 1733 patented 300 acres in Prince George County.[152] Another probable descendant, Thomas Pistole, appeared on the Pitsylvania List of tithables for 1767 as a non-propertyholder.[153]

Already on the headright lists for 1636 two observations can be made: 1) The proportion of persons with Italian names in the total number of headrights is infinitesimally small, and 2) There is a noticeable gravitation of those with Italian names toward the southern bank of the lower James — to the region which would comprise the counties (moving up-river) of Princess Anne, Norfolk, Nansemond, Isle of Wight, Surry, and Prince George — and to the two counties comprising the Eastern Shore, Northampton and Accomack.

[142] Arthur Percival Newton, *The Colonizing Activities of the English Puritans* (New Haven: Yale University Press, 1914), p. 175.

[143] N.M. Nugent, *Cavaliers and Pioneers*, I, 39.

[144] G.C. Greer, *Virginia Immigrants*, p. 6.

[145] N.M. Nugent, *Cavaliers and Pioneers*, I, 42.

[146] G.C. Greer, *Virginia Immigrants*, p. 66.

[147] *Ibid.*, p. 203; N.M. Nugent, *Cavaliers and Pioneers*, I, 51; *VMHB*, VI (July, 1898), 92.

[148] *VMHB*, V (October, 1897), 214.

[149] *VMHB*, II (October, 1894), 205-216.

[150] *VMHB*, III (April, 1896), 427.

[151] G.C. Greer, *Virginia Immigrants*, p. 260, *VMHB*, V (January, 1898), 339.

[152] Land Office Catalog, Virginia State Library.   [153] *VMHB*, XVIV (April, 1916), 187.

For 1637, the headright lists record the arrival of Thomas Attera (county not specified),[154] Anthony Luco (James City County),[155] and Joseph Crosia (Norfolk County).[156] The *Tristram and Jane* brought John Trevone, about whom nothing is known other than that he was listed as a servant,[157] Roger Shillito, whose services were sold to one Thomas Maleigh for 500 pounds of tobacco,[158] and Richard Nero and Christopher Gosse (Henrico County).[159] Others of this surname (Gosse) were Richard (Norfolk County) in 1644 and Edmond (New Kent County) in 1658.[160]

The next year, 1638, saw the arrival of Michael Cassino (James City County)[161], John Averine (Charles City County),[162] and Anthony Reboore (Rebore?) (James City County).[163] In 1639, Allen Sadone was brought to James City County.[164]

In that same year, Mr. Joseph Salmone, who must already have spent some time in the colony, was appointed one of the three "viewers" of the tobacco crop for farmers and plantations "from the Rudd Point to the head of Pagan Pond Creek",[165] a ten-mile riverbank section of Isle of Wight County. In 1641 (the name spelled Salmon but still with the "Mr.") he represented Isle of Wight County in the Assembly and was appointed acting commander of the county militia.[166]

---

[154] N.M. Nugent, *Cavaliers and Pioneers*, I, 62; *VMHB*, VII (October, 1899), 195. Although the headright was not always taken in the county in which it was granted, it would seem reasonable that in most (or many) cases the person "brought in" to the colony could be identified with the county for which the "right" was given. Acting on this assumption, in most cases, this identification will be given — unless an explanatory note is made.

[155] G.C. Greer, *Virginia Immigrants*, p. 211.

[156] *Ibid.*, p. 83; N.M. Nugent, *Cavaliers and Pioneers*, I, 67.

[157] "Accompts of the *Tristam and Jane*", edited by Martha W. Hiden, *VMHB*, 62 (October, 1954), 430: same document with same editor in Michael Tepper, ed., *New World Immigrants*, 2 vols. (Baltimore: Geneaological Publishing Co., Inc., 1979), I, 88.

[158] M.W. Hiden, ed., "Accompts", in M. Tepper, ed., *Immigrants*, I, 88.

[159] N.M. Nugent, *Cavaliers and Pioneers*, I, 59; G.C. Greer, *Virginia Immigrants*, p. 238.

[160] *Ibid.*, I, 186, 385.   [161] G.C. Greer, *Immigrants*, p. 61.

[162] N.M. Nugent, *Cavaliers and Pioneers*, I, 86.

[163] *Ibid.*, I, 102. In this same year Henry Pace came to Accomack County. This seems to have been the first person in the colony to bear this name. Others, many of them large landholders (Land Office Catalog, Virginia State Library), came to Virginia until the eve of the American Revolution. This may have been the common English name, but it should also be pointed out that Pace (pronounced Pá-chee) is a common Italian name both in Italy and the United States.

[164] G.C. Greer, *Immigrants*, p. 288.

[165] "Viewers of Tobacco Crop, 1639", *VMHB*, V (October, 1897), 121.

[166] *Minutes of the Council and General Court of Virginia*, H.R. McIlwaine, ed., second ed. (Richmond: Virginia State Library, 1979), p. 474; *VMHB*, IX (July, 1901), 51. In 1779, a John Salmon was "appointed to let the building of a Prison, Stocks & Pillory" for Henry County. "Henry County Records of the Clerk's Office", *VMHB*, IX (January, 1902), 266. Salmone (with variants Salamone and Salmode) was an old

Also appearing in the record for this time was Marra Mello, who it would seem was in the timber business in Norfolk County. In a case in Lower Norfolk County Court in 1639, one Thomas Todd was ordered to pay Mello 200 pounds of tobacco "due him for his last years work".[167] On May 25, 1640, Mello was again in court, this time as a defendant on charges that he "hath uttered divers scandalous speeches against Agnes, the wife of John Holmes tending to her great defamation thereby". The court found in favor of Mrs. Holmes and ordered that "he [Mello] shall, the next Sunday upon his knees at the parish church...confess that he hath done her wrong and openly ask God and her [for] forgiveness".[168]

Assuming that Mr. Thomas Caussonne was of Italian origin rather than French, it may be noted that that gentleman was elected to the vestry of Lynhaven Parish of Lower Norfolk County in 1640.[169] William Nobli, regarding whose origins there can be little question, also came to Norfolk County in the same year.[170]

In 1642, Abraham Harmata and Anthony Ribore (also listed for 1650) came to Virginia counties not specified in the record.[171] In 1643, Mark Gina and Philip Barricole came to Norfolk County,[172] Roger Sillito to a county not indicated in the record,[173] and Christian Demacheto to Machjack Bay,[174] the arm of the Chesapeake on the Gloucester County peninsula between the York and Rappahannock Rivers. The next year, Richard Goste came to Lower Norfolk County[175] and Richard Pattica to Northampton,[176] while 1645 marked the arrival of John Chrisippe in Warwick County,[177] and 1646 that of Nicholas Iego in York County.[178]

Scotts spelling of Solomon. George F. Black, *The Surnames of Scotland: Their Origins, Meaning, and History* (New York: New York Public Library, 1946), p. 708. Since the Salmone mentioned here settled in Isle of Wight County, it will be assumed that the name is Italian rather than Scottish.

[167] Lower Norfolk County Records, 1636-1646, *VMHB*, XXXX (July, 1931), 244, 247.

[168] Lower Norfolk County Records, 1636-1646, *VMHB*, XL (January, 1932), 39. A Michael Mallo (note spelling) patented several tracts of land in Augusta County. Land Office Catalog, Virginia State Library.

[169] *Lower Norfolk County, Virginia, Antiquary*, I (1895), 140. Caussonne was obviously not a newcomer.

[170] G.C. Greer, *Immigrants*, p. 241.

[171] N.M. Nugent, *Cavaliers and Pioneers*, I, 136; G.C. Greer, *Immigrants*, p. 276. John Nemo, assuming that this is not a variant of Nimmo, came to Virginia in 1642 (*Ibid.*, 238). In the same year, William Pudivatte, who may have been French, patented 200 acres "upon a creek of the Pagan Bay". Virginia State Land Office, County Abstracts, Isle of Wight County. William Valentine patented land in Isle of Wight County in 1642. Land Office Catalog, Virginia State Library. *See also, Edward Pleasants Valentine Papers,* 4 vols. (Richmond: The Valentine Museum, [n.d.]), IV, 2324.

[172] N.M. Nugent, *Cavaliers and Pioneers*, I, 150; G.C. Greer, *Immigrants*, p. 128.

[173] G.C. Greer, *Immigrants*, p. 298.   [174] *Ibid.,* p. 93.   [175] *Ibid.,* p. 132.

[176] Land Certification for Northampton County, *VMHB*, XXXVIII (January, 1920), 145. In 1691, a Thomas Pettice patented 93 acres in Rappahannock County. Land Office Catalog, Virginia State Library.

[177] G.C. Greer, *Immigrants*, p. 66.   [178] N.M. Nugent, *Cavaliers and Pioneers*, I, 164.

These immigrants of Italian extraction were small people who achieved little worldly success, died early, left no progeny for the record, or were quickly absorbed into the mainstream of the Virginia population without leaving a trace of their Italian origin, however distant that origin may have been in England.[179] Such, however, was not the case with Robert Taliaferro, a young man with a considerable amount of financial capital, who arrived in Virginia sometime about 1646.

Robert Taliaferro was the grandson of Bartholomew Taliaferro (Tagliafero), a subject of the Duke of Venice, who in 1562 paid 20s. for Letters of Denization in London. Although Bartholomew Taliaferro was a member of the family of court musicians by that name, Francis Taliaferro, Bartholomew's son by his wife Joane Lane, appears in the record as a yeoman of Bethnal Green in Stepney, County Middlesex. It was Robert Taliaferro, Francis' son by his wife Bennett Haie, who began the long line of one of Virginia's most distinguished families.[180]

Robert Taliaferro's name (and it was always pronounced "Toll-ver") first appears in the Virginia records when, on November 1, 1647, he, as a young man of 21 years, witnessed the will of Robert Meeke of York County.[181] In 1651, Taliaferro, with Samuel Salate, patented 800 acres in Gloucester County. In 1661, he patented an additional 900 Gloucester County acres in that part of Rappahannock County which would later become Caroline and Spotsylvania. In 1673, he would add 739 additional acres in Old Rappahannock.[182]

Meanwhile, Robert Taliaferro had married Sarah Grimes, daughter of the Reverend Charles Grimes, an Anglican priest of York County. The couple had one daughter, Catherine, who married Captain John Battaile, and four sons, Robert, Jr., Francis, John and Richard.[183] The lands accumulated by the first Robert were passed on to the sons, each of whom married leading "old" Virginia families, and each added, by marriage or purchase, to the family landholdings. In 1704, in Essex County alone, Francis was listed as holding 1,300 acres, Charles with 300 acres, and John with 2,000 acres.[184] Jackson Turner Main, in a most careful survey of wealth distribution in post-Revolutionary Virginia, lists the one hundred largest landholders and/or wealthiest individuals

---

[179] Philip Alexander Bruce, *Social Life of Virginia in the Seventeenth Century* (Williamstown, Massachusetts: Corner House Publishers, reprint of 1968), Pp. 250-251.

[180] The Taliaferro genealogy has been the subject (and victim) of much fanciful speculation, and most of the older Virginia genealogical citations are totally worthless. The most authoritative work is by Sir Anthony Wagner, K.C.V.O. (Garter King of Arms) and F.S. Andrus, "The Origins of the Family of Taliaferro", *VMHB*, 77 (January, 1969), 22-25. Witnesses to the will of Bartholomew Taliaferro (May 3, 1602) were Jerome Lopez, Pompilio Gaetani, Henry Valisi, and William Parkyns. *Ibid.,* p. 25.

[181] *Ibid.,* p. 23.

[182] Land Office Catalog, Virginia State Library.

[183] *VMHB*, XXVII (April, 1919), 185.

[184] T.J. Wertenbaker, *The Planters of Colonial Virginia*, p. 239. *C.f.* Virginia State Land Office, County Abstracts, Isle of Wight and Elizabeth City Counties for post-1704 holdings.

for the 1780s. Included in the "Hundred" is Richard Taliaferro, with 5,300 acres in James City, Brunswick, and Dinwiddie Counties, 102 slaves, 27 horses, and 141 head of cattle.[185]

The Taliaferros were, to say the least, biologically prolific. Families were large, and sons and daughters continued the precedent set by the sons of Robert "the immigrant" in marrying well. Even the most cursory examination of Virginia genealogical tables will strongly suggest that any white Virginian having Virginian ancestry of at least three generations will be in some way related to the Taliaferros.[186]

In the Taliaferro family, the women were noted for their beauty and the men for what seems to have been, generation after generation, unusual talent. Taliaferros served as representatives in the House of Burgesses, as county sheriffs, as churchwardens, as leading supporters of the College of William and Mary and, as the Revolution approached, members of the county Committees of Safety.[187] During the Revolution, Taliaferros served by the dozen in the Continental Army and the Virginia militia. Among those were Colonel Richard, who fell in the Battle of Guilford Court House in North Carolina, Lieutenant Colonel William R., Captain Benjamin, subaltern to General George Washington, and Nicolas, second lieutenant in the Virginia Sixth Regiment, on down to the Richard Taliaferro who marched as a private under General George Rogers Clark in the conquest of the Illinois Country.[188]

The American Revolution is a long way from the English Civil War which was raging when the first Taliaferro arrived in Virginia. Despite the facts that in England Cavaliers were fighting Roundheads, both Archbishop Laud and King Charles I would be executed, and the Puritans would come into full control and completely outlaw the Church of England, migration to Virginia continued without interruption. Nor did the take-over of the Virginia government by a Puritan expedition from Cromwellian England seem to have any effect. Thomas Crecro of Northampton County was, incidentally, one of the signers of the articles of surrender for the Eastern Shore.[189] The proportion of those Italian

[185] Jackson T. Main, "The One Hundred", *WMQ*, Third Series, XI (July, 1954), 367ff., esp. 382.

[186] Some of the Early Marriage Licenses of Orange County, *WMQ*, First Series, IV (October, 1895), 60, 92. *The Taliaferro Family Chart*, compiled by W.B. Groarty (Falls Church, VA: the compiler, 1928) gives full details.

[187] Philip Alexander Bruce, *Institutional History of Virginia in the Seventeenth Century*, 2 vols. (New York: G.P. Putnam's Sons, 1910), I, 601-602; Some of the Early Marriage Licenses of Orange County, *WMQ*, First Series, IV (October, 1895), 92; Journals of the Meetings of the President and Masters of William and Mary College, *WMQ*, First Series, IV (October, 1895), 130, 188; *WMQ*, First Series, VI, (April, 1897), 102, 104, 105, 188, 247.

[188] Virginia Officers and Men in the Continental Line, *VMHB*, II (January, 1895), 244, 357-359; Michael A. Musmanno, *The Story of the Italians in America* (Garden City, N.Y.: Doubleday and Co., 1965), Pp. 8, 54n; "The Illinois Regiment and the Northwest Territory", *VMHB*, I (October, 1893), 134.

[189] Surrender of the Inhabitants of Northampton County, Virginia, to the Commonwealth of England, March, 1651, *The Virginia Historical Register*, I (October, 1848), 165.

names coming to Virginia remained about the same as it had been during the earlier decades.

In 1647, James Saiferne came to York County as an indentured servant, and Thomas Bremo acquired a landholding by purchase in the same county. Saiferne appeared in no subsequent records, but Bremo did, being "detained" by the sheriff several times for drunkenness. Fortunately, however, he reformed, as by 1651 he had acquired the title of "Captain" and patented some 1,500 acres of land in the Mockjack Bay region of Gloucester County. The name, too, underwent change (if not reform), with a transition from Bremo, to Bremore, to Bremor, to Bremow.[190]

And still they came — John Carliere, Ann Virose, and John Carassue in 1648,[191] and Richard Tonne, Thomas Tuata, James Millacha, and Saliman De Carvolco in 1649.[192] Then came the flood year of 1650 with the arrival of Edward Attore,[193] John Cabboe (Cabbore),[194] Arthur Cannanna,[195] Symon Bargine,[196] Hugh Michalla,[197] John Peio,[198] William Farra,[199] John Tero,[200] and Babtisto Carbone[201] (or Baptisio Corbone).[202] At this point it might be mentioned in passing that the mother of Isaac Collier (Collyer) of York County, whose will was probated on January 8, 1649/50, was Anna Semiliano and that his sister, presumably still in England, had married one Vincentio Malo.[203]

In 1651, Jane Lectra and John Gesorroro came to Northampton County on the Eastern Shore,[204] and John Blitto was one of a band of 42 servants including nine blacks and one "Syon the Turk" brought to satisfy headrights for a tract of 2,104 acres in Northumberland County known as Doggs Island.[205]

James Muskatina was entered as a headright to Charles River (York) County in 1652, and his name also appears in the 1654 list for a tract in Gloucester County.[206] In 1652, John Cavide was listed for Gloucester County[207] and Philip

[190] Notes from the Records of York County, WMQ, First Series, XXIII (July, 1914), 11; ibid. (January, 1915), 204; ibid. (April, 1915), 274; William Cabell Moore, "Gen. John Hartwell Cocke of Bremo", WMQ, Second Series, XIII (October, 1933), 210; G.C. Greer, Immigrants, p. 288; N.M. Nugent, Cavaliers and Pioneers, I, 222, 341; Virginia State Land Office, County Abstracts, Gloucester County.

[191] N.M. Nugent, Cavaliers and Pioneers, I, 180, 182; G.C. Greer, Immigrants, Pp. 59, 338. Carliere came to Lower Norfolk County, Ibid., p. 59.

[192] Ibid., Pp. 93, 300, 333; N.M Nugent, Cavaliers and Pioneers, I, 179, 181, 186.

[193] N.M. Nugent, Cavaliers and Pioneers, I, 200.   [194] Ibid., I, 194.

[195] Ibid., I, 194.   [196] Ibid., I, 208.   [197] G.C. Greer, Immigrants, p. 224.

[198] Ibid., p. 254.   [199] Ibid., p. 111.   [200] N.M. Nugent, Cavaliers and Pioneers, I, 207.

[201] G.C. Greer, Immigrants, p. 78.   [202] N.M. Nugent, Cavaliers and Pioneers, I, 198.

[203] Will of Isaac Collyer. Probated January 8, 1649/50, in London, England, VMHB, XVIII (July, 1900), 304-305, 305n.

[204] Land Certificates for Northampton County, VMHB, XXXVIII (January, 1920), 147; N.M. Nugent, Cavaliers and Pioneers, I, 216.

[205] Ibid., I, 218.   [206] Ibid., I, 272, 302; G.C. Greer, Immigrants, 236.   [207] Ibid., p. 62.

Barricole for Northampton County.[208] The same name, unless this is Barricole, *Junior*, was in the 1643 lists for Lower Norfolk,[209] which could mean that either headright credit was given for a return trip or this was a "padding" of the list of headrights.

For 1653, the headrights carried the names of Mary Cesar (Charles City County), Ann Simco and Thomas Treplana (on the roster of William Clairborne who was then operating a trading post on the site of present Hampton), William Valeveo (county not designated), Will Mattro (Charles City County), and Thomassen Madero (York County).[210] Later Virginians bearing similar (variant?) surnames were James Maddero, an Isle of Wight County landholder and loyal supporter of Governor Berkeley during Bacon's Rebellion of 1676,[211] and those following whose wills were probated in the counties and years given: John Madera (King George, 1725), Sarah Maddera (Surry, 1767), William (Surry, 1773), Zadirich Maddero (Surry, 1774), Christopher Maddera (1782), and Joseph Maddery (Isle of Wight, 1781).[212] Later Cesars, although not necessarily related to this Mary, were John Cesar, who in 1707 was appointed to the Commission of the Peace for King William County,[213] and Darby Ceasar (note spelling), who in 1724 patented 144 acres in the same county.[214]

The year 1654 brought William Perrigoe (Perrigo) and Marke Provo to counties unnamed in the record and Johanna Stella to York County.[215] In that year or shortly thereafter, Ann Ceco and Edward Ilia were ordered to be sent as convicts from Bristol, England, to Virginia,[216] although there is no record of their arrival in the colony. Also, in 1654, one Nicholas Vincento (probably no relation to the Vincentio of glassblower fame) died in Norfolk County.[217]

In 1655, the following persons satisfied headrights: Jane Nevera, John Dozo,

[208] N.M. Nugent, *Cavaliers and Pioneers*, I, 264.

[209] *See above*. In 1652, James Longe, although it is uncertain whether he was of Italian extraction, patented over 500 acres in Nansemond County. Land Office Catalog, Virginia State Library.

[210] G.C. Greer, *Immigrants*, Pp. 63, 214, 216, 298, 332, 336; N.M. Nugent, *Cavaliers and Pioneers*, I, 257; Lyon Gardiner Tyler, *The Cradle of the Republic* (Richmond: The Hermitage Press, 1906), p. 247.

[211] John Bennett Boddie, *Seventeenth Century Isle of Wight County, Virginia* (Chicago: Law Publishing Co., 1938), Pp. 161, 592. Simcoe was an old English Northumberland name, but that is not necessarily the same as the "Simco" given here.

[212] *Virginia Wills and Abstracts 1632-1800, An Index*, compiled by Clayton Torrence (Richmond: William Byrd Press, [n.d.]), p. 277.

[213] *Executive Journal of the Council of Colonial Virginia*, II, 147.

[214] Land Office Catalog, Virginia State Library.

[215] G.C. Greer, *Immigrants* Pp. 256, 268; N.M. Nugent, *Cavaliers and Pioneers*, I, 313.

[216] R. Hargreaves-Mowderly, *Bristol and America: A Record of the First Settlers in the Colonies of North America, 1654-1685* (Balitmore: Genealogical Publishing Co., Inc., 1978), Pp. 35, 86. On the subject of transportation of criminals, *see below*.

[217] *Virginia Wills and Administrations, 1632-1800*, p. 435.

John Malladone, and Carona Cornelia in Northampton County,[218] Gespan Vigeo in Lancaster County,[219] John Mottio in Gloucester,[220] and Hugon Veceto in Isle of Wight.[221] One of the most interesting entries in the land records is for the 300 acres in Northampton County patented on October 2, 1655, by John Westlocke for transporting 6 persons: Rose Lyna (Lina), Arthur Lina, and Mary Lina (apparently a family), and John Holmes, William Mees, and Jane Doe.[222] For 1656, the headright lists carry the names of Francis Croffa (Nansemond County), Ann Pettito (Northumberland County), and Susan Cortero (James City County).[223] Roro Molletta (Northumberland County) seems to have been the only arrival for 1657.[224]

Although the date of his arrival in Virginia is unknown, Dr. John Clulo began a brief medical practice in York County about 1658. Nothing is known of his medical training, and he is remembered solely for charging what were regarded as exorbitant fees for administering enimas.[225]

Meanwhile, the Commonwealth Period of English history was drawing to a close. Oliver Cromwell died on September 3, 1659, and he was succeeded by his son Richard as Lord Protector. By this time, however, English bellies were full of Puritanism, and the return of the Stuart monarchs in the person of Charles II early in 1660 was welcomed both in England and Virginia.

It would be altogether impossible to make any correlation between the events taking place in England and the coming to Virginia of persons bearing Italian surnames, just as it is impossible to make any meaningful overall generalizations regarding all migration to the colony.[226] For whatever it may be worth, however, neither the beginning nor the end of the English Civil War seems to have had an effect upon the migration to Virginia of Englishmen of Italian extraction, as 1658 saw the arrival in Virginia of Peter Arbo, 1659 that of Gihelinus Varlee, 1660 that of Christo Massoine, 1661 that of Thomas Dulano, and 1662, John Farro. In 1663 Teage Matarta was "headrighted" in Accomack County and Thomas Dinto in Lower Norfolk County.[227] In that same year, or shortly

---

[218] G.C. Greer, *Immigrants*, p. 98, 238; N.M. Nugent, *Cavaliers and Pioneers*, I, 307.

[219] *Ibid.*, I, 311.   [220] *Ibid.*, I, 307; G.C. Greer, *Immigrants*, 222.

[221] N.M. Nugent, *Cavaliers and Pioneers*, I, 322.

[222] *Ibid.*, I, 324. A James Lina came to New Kent County in 1682. *Ibid.*, I, 228.

[223] *Ibid.*, I, 338-339; G.C. Greer, *Immigrants*, p. 84.

[224] N.M. Nugent, *Cavaliers and Pioneers*, I, 357.

[225] Wyndham B. Blanton, M.D., *Medicine in Virginia in the Seventeenth Century* (Richmond: The William Byrd Press, Inc., 1930), Pp. 135-136, 265; Thomas P. Hughes, *Medicine in Colonial Virginia, 1607-1709* [No. 21 in Jamestown 350th Anniversary *History Booklets*] (Williamsburg: Virginia's 350th Anniversary Celebration Corporation, 1957), p. 66.

[226] The immigration records based entirely on headright grants given in N.M. Nugent, *Cavaliers and Pioneers*, shows no discernable change.

[227] R. Hargreaves-Mowderley, *Bristol and America*, Pp. 117, 123.

thereafter, Thomas Bindoco and Pacco Bellico, both convicts, were sent from Bristol to Virginia.[228] In 1664, Jone (Joane) Vina and Jacaminta Bodella were entered into the Accomack County lists and Mary Fristo on those of Rappahannock and Northumberland Counties.[229] The Accomack County records for 1644 also show that Owen Colona was one of 30 persons brought by Mr. John West for claims to 1,500 acres on the Eastern Shore.[230]

Owen Colona was descended from the old and famous Italian Colona family,[231] but nothing is known of how long his immediate forebears had lived in England. Nor is it certain that he remained in Virginia long after his first arrival, as he was listed in 1672 as one of 91 persons named by Edmond Scarborough for 4,500 acres in Northampton.[232] Scarborough, a large and influential magnate of the Eastern Shore, had the reputation of being somewhat less than totally scrupulous,[233] and he probably was not above padding his headright lists. Or — Colona may have been in Scarborough's employ and had been in charge of a direct recruiting trip to England. Whatever may have been the case, Colona had both resources and ambition, bringing his family to the colony and quickly acquired landholdings in his own right. By 1704, Owen Colona held 500 acres in Accomack County, and William Colona (a son) held 400 acres in Gloucester County.[234]

The restoration of the Stuart monarchy marked a new development in the nature of migration from England to Virginia. Although some of the individuals already mentioned have been indicated as transported criminals, it is entirely possible that some of those not so indicated may also have been sent to Virginia as convicts, and certainly, as we will see, the number of transported convicts increased greatly after 1660.

The idea of "transportation" was not a new one, having its origin in an Elizabethan Act of Parliament of 1597 which provided for the banishment from the kingdom of rogues and vagabonds. Although the vast majority of those coming to Virginia during the pre-Revolution years were either farmers or skilled laborers (with common laborers in a small minority),[235] Edward D. Neill,

[228] N.M. Nugent, *Cavaliers and Pioneers*, I, 430, 452.   [229] *Ibid.*, I, 454.

[230] Ralph T. Whitelaw, *Virginia's Eastern Shore: A History of Northampton and Accomack Counties*, 2 vols. (Gloucester, Massachusetts: Peter Smith, 1968), I, 651.

[231] N.M. Nugent, *Cavaliers and Pioneers*, II, 106.

[232] Sandra Lee Rux, "Edmund Scarburgh, a Biography: 1617-1671" (Unpublished M.A. thesis, Trinity College, Hartford, Connecticut, 1980), *Passim*.

[233] Annie Laurie Wright Smith, comp., *The Quit Rent of Virginia* (n.p., 1957), Pp. 20-21.

[234] Mildred Campbell, "Social Origins of Some Early Americans", in James Morton Smith, ed., *Seventeenth-Century America: Essays in Colonial History* (Chapel Hill: University of North Carolina Press, 1959), p. 73; David W. Falenson, *White Servitude in Colonial America* (London: Cambridge University, 1981), Pp. 34-64.

[235] Edward D. Neill, *Virginia Vetusta* (Albany, N.Y.: Joel Murrill's Sons, 1885), p. 101.

in what was an obvious overstatement, remarked that "From the beginning of the plantation in Virginia, it had been the policy of the Company to send thither their poor children, and those who did not stand well in England".[236] And to make his point, Neill gives examples of cases of deported convicts and kidnapped children.[237]

"Spiriting" (or kidnapping) children for sale to Virginia was not particularly common, but opportunities to engage in the practice certainly existed. Although "spiriting" was forbidden by law, the law does not seem to have been strictly enforced, and even when fines were imposed, they were seldom for more than a shilling, making, in fact, the stealing of a child no more serious an offense than the stealing of a horse. Sadly, too, it must be noted that the English records are replete with examples of parents or other relatives who actually sold children for transportation to the colonies.[238] Only one possible case of spiriting seems relevant to this study. On May 9, 1677 in Middlesex County, "James Peerdo",[239] servant to John Batchelder "coming into this country in the ship *Raleigh* is adjudged eleven years of age".[240]

If "spiriting" were not common, "transportation" for criminal offenses was. Peter Wilson Coldham, the leading scholar on the subject of "transportation", insists that the number of those "transported" increased steadily after 1660, reaching its peak at the end of the century.[241] Perhaps the oft-quoted "Luttrell Diary" entry of November, 1692, is a gross overstatement, but in view of the fact that it has been so often used to stress the extent of certain types of deviant conduct, it may well be quoted here: "That a ship lay in Leith going for Virginia, on board which the Magistrates had ordered 50 lewd women out of the houses of correction, and 30 others who walked the streets after 10 at night."[242] The fact that Leith is a Scottish port seems not to have deterred those who have quoted the diary and applied it to the England-Virginia migration. Nevertheless, it does point up the fact of female transportation *a la* Moll Flanders in Daniel Defoe's famous novel.

Certainly noticeable in the post-Restoration records is the large number of women and men specifically designated as convicts, but the record, so far as an Italian presence is concerned, does little to suggest that persons of Italian

---

[236] *Ibid.*, pp. 102ff.

[237] Peter Wilson Coldham, "The 'Spiriting' of London Children to Virginia: 1648-1685", *VMHB*, 83 (July, 1975), 280ff.

[238] *See below* for Peerdo (Pardo, Purdue) family.

[239] *Edward Pleasants Valentine Papers*, I, 179.

[240] Peter Wilson Coldham, *English Convicts in Colonial America*, 2 vols. (New Orleans: Polyanthos, 1974-1976), I, x.

[241] Quoted in Neill, *Virginia Vetusta*, p. 103.

[242] Catto (note spelling) was a Scottish name common in Aberdeenshire. G.F. Black, *Surnames of Scotland*, p. 143.

extraction were sent as convicts in any disproportionate numbers. Priscilla Cotto (Colto or Cutto, as it also appears in the record)[243] is entered for Henrico County in 1665[244] and for Stafford County in 1666.[245] Susan Tessero was entered for Accomack County in 1667.[246] In neither case, however, is there any indication that "transportation" for criminal offense was involved, even though the word "transportation" was used.

Nevertheless, convicts were coming to Virginia, and, in 1670, the Virginia General Court ordered that no more convicts or felons be sent. This act was approved by the Privy Council in England, but in 1718, Parliament reversed this order and passed an act requiring all colonies to accept all transported felons, whether they wanted them or not.[247]

However many convicts came, this same post-Restoration period saw the arrival in Virginia of persons of Italian extraction who were eminently "respectable", and some of these began dynasties which, like the earlier Taliaferros, were to become leaders in the colony and early nation.

Perhaps the best known of these families was that which later came to be known as Lanier, the most famous member being Sidney Lanier, the mid-nineteenth century lyric poet. The Laniers were long assumed to have been French, and even the authoritative *New Grove Dictionary of Music and Musicians* refers to them as an "English family of musicians of French descent".[248] The Leneares were indeed a musical family, but careful genealogical study in the early twentieth century has positively established the family as Italian, with the first representatives of the family, Nicolo and Jerome, going to England in the days of Elizabeth I as court musicians and painters.[249]

John Leneare, the immigrant, came to Virginia in the mid 1660s, took the rebel side in Bacon's Rebellion in 1676,[250] and in 1682 patented, with one Peter Wycke, a tract of land on the north side of the James River in Charles City County.[251] In 1728, Nicholas, a descendant of John Leneare (the name here is spelled Lanear) patented land in Brunswick County,[252] and in 1764 one John (spelling his name in the original Italianate form of Leneare) patented 78 acres of land in the same county.[253]

[243] N.M Nugent, *Cavaliers and Pioneers*, I, 535, 563. [244] *Ibid.*, II, 24. [245] *Ibid.*, II, 24.

[246] Fairfax Harrison, "When the Convicts Came", *VMHB*, XXX (July, 1922), 250ff. [247] X, 454.

[248] Reginold M. Glencross, "Virginia Gleanings in England", *VMHB*, XXX (July, 1924), 261n. by George Cole Scott.

[249] Lena E. Jackson and Aubrey Starke, "New Light on the Ancestry of Sidney Lanier", *VMHB*, XVIII (April, 1935), 227.

[250] He was a minor participant and there is no record of his having been punished for his part in the uprising.

[251] Virginia State Land Office, County Abstracts, Charles City County.

[252] Virginia State Land Office, County Abstracts, Brunswick County.

[253] Land Office Catalog, Virginia State Library.

Another family line began with John Cannida who came to Gloucester County in March, 1666/7,[254] or John Connadra who is listed in New Kent County for February, 1673/4.[255] The will of John Canada was probated in Westmoreland in 1702, for Samuel Cannadey in Isle of Wight County in 1711, and for William Canada in Bedford County in 1775.[256] In 1778, a William Cannada purchased 385 acres in Bedford County for £38.10.0.[257]

Much better known was the family which began in the late 1660s with Philip and Thomas Pardo, either brothers or father and son,[258] in Isle of Wight County,[259] who, by the end of the seventeenth century, had acquired considerable landholdings.[260] The family also seems to have had resources other than in land, as in 1677, Philip Pardo gave security in several matters relating to the settlement of estates in Isle of Wight County.[261] Those of successive generations left small estates, and in these wills and inventories an interesting change of name can be traced. The inventory of the estate of the first Philip Pardo was recorded in 1678. In 1720 Philip Pardue's inventory was recorded in Isle of Wight, and in 1794, the will of Josiah Perdue was probated in Chesterfield County.[262] One must wonder how this reputable family reacted to the arrival in Virginia of one Elizabeth Pardoe who in 1732 was sentenced in London to "transportation" for fourteen years.[263]

The name of the Gunsalvo family underwent similar transformation following the arrival in 1682 of Lorenzo, Sarah, and Thomas, listed for headright claim in Nansemond County.[264] We know little of this family other than that shortly after its arrival, the father, listed as living in Nansemond County, was awarded 600 pounds of tobacco for the capture of three runaway servants.[265] Eighteenth-century members of the family modified the spelling, as indicated in wills and

[254] N.M. Nugent, Cavaliers and Pioneers, II, 12.

[255] Ibid., II, 149.

[256] Virginia Wills and Administrations, 1632-1800, Pp. 69-70.

[257] Edward Pleasants Valentine Papers, II, 958.

[258] The record is not clear as to the relationship.

[259] Elsdon C. Smith, New Dictionary of American Family Names, p. 387; "Pardoe, Pardo (Sp. It.). One who had gray hair; descendant of Pardo, a pet form of Leopardo (Lion)". "Sp." here means Spanish, "It." here means Italian.

[260] John Bennett Boddie, Seventeenth Century Isle of Wight County, Virginia, Pp. 567, 598, 640, 650. Curiously, however, the Rent Roll of 1704-1705 lists only Philip with 100 acres; T.J. Wertenbaker, The Planters of Colonial Virgina, p. 195.

[261] Edward Pleasants Valentine Papers, II, 597.

[262] Virginia Wills and Estates, 1632-1800, Pp. 324, 331.

[263] P.W. Coldham, English Convicts, II, 112. A Mary Pardo was sentenced in 1747, but there is no record of her arrival in Virginia. Ibid., II, 112.

[264] N.M. Nugent, Cavaliers and Pioneers, II, 245-246.

[265] Journal of the House of Burgesses of Virginia, 1659/60-1693, p. 178.

inventories of estates: William Consoul (1753), William Consalvo (1758), Henry Consalvo (1764), and John Consaul (1774), all of Prince Anne County, and Charles Consolvo (1768) of Norfolk County.[266]

The Parmento family of Isle of Wight County presents problems of a genealogical nature which are not easily solved. The first members of the family came to Virginia probably in the mid- or late-1670s. In 1679, Mrs. Mary Parmento and Thomas Gereise entered into a marriage contract.[267] This Mary was doubtless a widow with one or more sons, as a John Permento (note spelling) appeared in the records as a grand juror for Isle of Wight County in 1692,[268] and the name of Nathaniel Permento came into the land records during the 1690s.[269] John died on June 27, 1715,[270] and although his will was not probated until 1718,[271] Mary Parmento, probably the widow, married a John Murry late in 1715.[272] Nathaniel died in 1721, and in his will the name is spelled Parmenter. The name of John Parmentoe appears as witness to a will dated March 20, 1735.[273]

The Via family was the one family of which the main line retained the original spelling, although it was, of all families of Italian origin, one of the most geographically mobile. The first Virginia Via was probably Amor (or Amos) Via, one of 14 persons brought to New Kent County by John Webb in 1677.[274] Although Vias do not appear again in the records for almost a century, in 1768, a ropemaker of this name was operating in Norfolk. This man (first name not recorded) took a strong stand against rioters who were opposed to smallpox innoculation during an epidemic of that disease in Norfolk.[275] In the Revolutionary period Vias were living in Amherst, Henrico, and Albemarle Counties.[276]

One last family of Italian extraction dating from this period was that beginning with Thomas Guanto whose name appears on the 1687 headright list for 1,075

[266] Virginia Wills and Administrations, 1632-1800, p. 98.

[267] Blanche Adams Chapman, ed., Isle of Wight County Marriages, 1628-1800 (n.p., 1933), p. 21.

[268] Isle of Wight County Records, VMHB, First Series, VII (April, 1899), 259.

[269] J.B. Boddie, Seventeenth Century Isle of Wight County, Virginia, p. 623.

[270] B.A. Chapman, ed., Wills and Administrations of Isle of Wight County, Virginia, 1647-1800, I, 81.

[271] Ibid., I, 87. The name is spelled Parmentoe in the will.

[272] B.A. Chapman, Isle of Wight County Marriages, 1628-1800, p. 37.

[273] Ibid., II, 15; B.A. Chapman, ed., Wills and Administrations of Isle of Wight County, Virginia, 1647-1800, II, 79.

[274] N.M. Nugent, Cavaliers and Pioneers, II, 179.

[275] Patrick Henderson, "Smallpox and Patriotism: The Norfolk Riots, 1768-1769", VMHB, 73 (October, 1965), 417-418.

[276] Virginia Wills and Abstracts, 1632-1800, Passim; Abstracts of Wills, Inventories, and Administration Accounts of Albemarle County, Virginia, (1748-1800), and Amherst County, Virginia (1761-1800), compiled by J. Estelle Stewart King (Beverly Hills: Pub. by the compiler, 1940), p. 15.

acres "back of Col. William Byrd's land at Falling Creek",[277] just down the James River from the present site of Richmond. This seems to be a clear-cut case of names entered on headright lists for land in one location, while the individuals were located elsewhere, as the next appearance of the name (with variant spelling) was the will of John Gurnto probated in Princess Anne County in 1694.[278] The family thereafter was solidly based in Princess Anne, and although William Grinto seems to have been the only large landholder (with 650 acres listed for 1704),[279] Princess Anne probate records carry the names of Peter (1722), William (1734), John (1754), William., Jr., spelled Gronto (1789), and John (1790).[280] One of the Johns was listed as holding 35 acres and one slave in 1774.[281]

But not all of those of Italian extraction who came to Virginia during this period came in families — or even began families, and here again must be mentioned those who came as individuals and who appear but briefly in the record. Those coming to satisfy headright claims were: George Fardinando (Lower Norfolk)[282] and Benjamin Vintua (Henrico)[283] in 1665; Gerat Christi (Stafford)[284], Toby Nichola (Nansemond)[285], and Mary Blanto (Accomack)[286] in 1666; Symon Balono (Henrico)[287], Rosse Gussiso,[288] and Vincent De Loppo (Middlesex)[289] in 1667; Andrew Abrega (Accomack) in 1668;[290] John Blanto (Isle of Wight)[291] in 1669; David Salmo (or Salino) (Accomack)[292] and Richard Albane (Rappahannock)[293] in 1670; William Trevisa (Northampton)[294] and William Bosca (Northampton)[295] in 1671; William Pallma (Northampton),[296] Charles Agore (Northampton),[297] Thomas Colle (Gloucester),[298] Anthony

---

[277] N.M. Nugent, *Cavaliers and Pioneers*, II, 316.

[278] *Virginia Wills and Administrations, 1632-1800*, p. 185.

[279] T.J. Wertenbaker, *The Planters of Colonial Virginia*, p. 206. William died in 1706, and in the inventory of his estate, the name is spelled "Grinta".

[280] *Virginia Wills and Administrations*, p. 176.

[281] *Lower Norfolk County, Virginia, Aniquary*, I (1895), 6.

[282] N.M. Nugent, *Cavaliers and Pioneers*, I, 445. The counties indicated here are for headright claims, not necessarily the county in which the individual located.

[283] *Ibid.*, I, 452.   [284] *Ibid.*, I, 546.

[285] *Ibid.*, I, 568. The name is spelled both Nichola and Nicholas in the same document.

[286] *Ibid.*, II, 7.   [287] *Ibid.*, II, 15.   [288] *Ibid.*, II, 135.   [289] *Ibid.*, II, 344.

[290] *Ibid.*, II, 48. Abrega is listed again in 1679 for a headright in Accomack County. *Ibid.*, II, 81.

[291] Probably the husband of Mary Blanto who came in 1666. *Ibid.*, II, 66.

[292] *Ibid.*, II, 81.   [293] *Ibid.*, II, 76.

[294] *Ibid.*, II, 94. A William Trevisa is listed again for Northampton County in 1673. *Ibid.*, II, 140.

[295] *Ibid.*, II, 94. A William Pasca is listed for Northampton County in 1673. *Ibid.*, II, 139.

[296] *Ibid.*, II, 106.   [297] *Ibid.*, II, 119.

[298] *Ibid.*, II, 18. A Robert Colle is listed for New Kent County for February, 1673/4, and a John Celli for Rappahannock County for May, 1679.

Rullo (Northampton),[299] and Elias Vergania (Northampton)[300] in 1672; John Carusue (Northampton),[301] and Rosse Gussio (Northampton),[302] in 1673; Robert Lambo (New Kent),[303] Joshua Esto (New Kent and Rappahannock),[304] and Jacob Flepo (New Kent),[305] in 1674; John Manzo (Accomack),[306] Emanuell Delannero (Accomack)[307] in 1675; Richard Vessi (Rappahannock)[308] in 1678; Walter Patso (New Kent)[309] in 1680; Walter Pascoe (New Kent)[310] in 1681; William Allingo (Isle of Wight)[311] and William Debora (King and Queen and Essex),[312] in 1683; James Seco (Rappahannock)[313] and Edward Folio (King and Queen and Essex),[314] in 1688; Mary Piccore (Charles City)[315] and Katherine Fillia (Norfolk)[316] in 1692; Mantidell Migro (Nansemond),[317] William and Alice Nutto (Nansemond),[318] and John and Sarah Sliddo (Nansemond)[319] in 1695; Elenor Cavano (Essex)[320] in 1696; John Susano (Essex),[321] and John Selmo (Essex),[322] in 1698; Fernando Mando (James City?),[323] and Walter Pasca (New Kent), in 1701; and Elizabeth Silvanne and Elliva Bricheno (King and Queen),[324] in 1702.

None of these listed individuals (or husband and wife teams) seems to have acquired property or left any mark in history. One individual, however, did, and that was John Babtista (or Baptista), who was brought to Virginia in 1672 as one of those named by Captain John West in a headright claim for 3,650 acres in Northampton County.[325]

Although Baptista had come to the colony as one of a large batch of individual servants, he seems to have acquired some property. When Bacon's Rebellion occurred in 1676, Baptista joined the rebel cause, becoming, in fact, one of Nathaniel Bacon's chief lieutenants. This is evidenced by the fact that he

[299] *Ibid.*, II, 115.   [300] *Ibid.*, II, 109.

[301] *Ibid.*, II, 139. A John Carassue has already been listed for 1648. *See above* and *Ibid.*, I, 180.

[302] *Ibid.*, II, 135.   [303] *Ibid.*, II, 143.

[304] *Ibid.*, II, 256.

[305] *Ibid.*, II, 144. In 1683, Jacob Fleepo patented 100 acres in New Kent County for transporting two persons (probably members of his family). *Ibid.*, II, 255. On December 7, 1674, one Nicholas Silverdo was charged by the justices of Northampton County with being the father of an illegitimate child. Silverdo posted bond but fled the country before he could be brought to trial. His name does not appear again in the Virginia records. T.H. Breen and Stephen Innes, *"Myne Owne Ground": Race and Freedom on Virginia's Eastern Shore* (New York: Oxford University Press, 1980), Pp. 104-105.

[306] N.M. Nugent, *Cavaliers and Pioneers*, II, 162.

[307] *Ibid.*, II, 174.   [308] *Ibid.*, II, 181.   [309] *Ibid.*, II, 210.   [310] *Ibid.*, III, 53.

[311] *Ibid.*, II, 254.   [312] *Ibid.*, III, 91.   [313] *Ibid.*, II, 328.   [314] *Ibid.*, III, 35.

[315] *Ibid.*, III, 103.   [316] *Ibid.*, III, 375.   [317] *Ibid.*, III, 5.   [318] *Ibid.*, III, 4.

[319] *Ibid.*, III, 5.

[320] *Ibid.*, III, 97. A John Cavenoe came to Isle of Wight County in 1714. *Ibid.*, III, 160.

[321] *Ibid.*, III, 21.   [322] *Ibid.*, III, 46.   [323] *Ibid.*, III, 52.   [324] *Ibid.*, III, 59.

[325] *Ibid.*, II, 104.

was specifically excluded, along with Bacon himself, from Governor Berkeley's general pardon and was sentenced to death on the charge of high treason.[326]

Along with one Drummond, identified in the records as "a Scotchman", Baptista was hanged just outside Jamestown.[327] The contemporary accounts however, are just a bit misleading as to Baptista's origin. Governor Berkeley, in his personal account of the Rebellion, blamed Drummond as much as Bacon for instigating the uprising, and he wrote that Drummond was hanged "with a common Frenchman, [and] that he had been very bloody".[328] Mrs. Ann Cotton, in *An Account of Our Late Trouble in Virginia*, wrote that Drummond was executed "with a Pittiful French man".[329] As "Baptista" is the Italian form, rather than the French, there can be little doubt as to his identity.

Apart from the headright lists, there are other contemporary evidences of the Italian presence. In 1665, one Dancie Attlo was granted 150 acres for "bringing in" three persons.[330] In 1666, Thomas Vantore (age 25) was involved in a lawsuit involving a personal debt.[331] In 1673 one Benonine Borace patented 944 acres in Lower Norfolk County.[332] In 1676, the wife of Giles Bristo received a bequest in the will of John Hardy of Isle of Wight County.[333] In 1679 the will of Edward Bechino was probated in Isle of Wight.[334] In 1682, Thomas Motro of New Kent County was paid 200 pounds of tobacco for "taking up" a runaway.[335] In 1684, Abraham Petto (age 21) was bound in England to serve John Williams of Virginia for four years.[336] In that same year, Thomas Allomaine patented 52 acres in Gloucester County.[337] In 1687, Mr. John Corperoe received a summons from the sheriff of Norfolk County to testify at James City in a case involving the seizure and condemnation of a cargo of black slaves brought on the ship *Societye* out of Bristol, England.[338] Although the context suggests that Corperoe

---

[326] Hening, *Statutes*, II, 370, 375.

[327] *Minutes of the Council and General Court of Virginia*, p. 454.

[328] William Berkeley, *A List of those that have been Executed for the Late Rebellion in Virginia*, in Peter Force, *Tracts*, I.

[329] In Force, *Tracts*, I.

[330] N.M. Nugent, *Cavaliers and Pioneers*, I, 541.

[331] Surry County Records, 1652-1684, Virginia State Library, Book I, p. 86.

[332] Land Office Catalog, Virginia State Library.

[333] *Edward Pleasants Valentine Papers*, II, 596.

[334] *Virginia Wills and Administrations, 1632-1800*, p. 28.

[335] *Journals of the House of Burgesses*, p. 180.

[336] Michael Ghirelli, *A List of Emigrants from England to America, 1682-1692* (Baltimore: Magna Carta Book Company, 1968), p. 64.

[337] Land Office Catalog, Virginia State Library.

[338] *Executive Journals of the Council of Colonial Virginia*, H.R. McIlwaine, ed., 5 vols. (Richmond: Virginia State Library, 1925-1945), I, 235-236.

might have been a ship captain, he was probably the John Corpero whose will was probated in Norfolk County in 1700, with the estate settled in Princess Anne the following year. Others bearing the variant name Corporew were William (will probated in Princess Anne in 1722), John (will probated in Norfolk County in 1749), a second John (will probated in Norfolk in 1769), and Thomas (will also probated in Norfolk County in 1796).[339]

In 1705, the will of Benjamin Burro was probated in Princess Anne.[340] In 1693, Enos Pollongi acquired a landholding of 450 acres near Lawson's Bay in Isle of Wight.[341] The will of Julian Martino was probated in Accomack County in 1696[342] and that of "the Widow Veste" in Norfolk County in 1699.[343]

This listing, tedious as it may have been for the reader, must be conclusive evidence of an Italian presence in seventeenth century Virginia, but we would wish for some more personal glimpse into the lives of those who pass before us as mere names on an official record!

[339] *Virginia Wills and Administrations, 1632-1800*, p. 98.

[340] *Ibid.*, p. 63.

[341] J.B. Boddie, *Seventeenth Century Isle of Wight*, Pp. 611-612.

[342] *Virginia Wills and Administrations, 1632-1800*, p. 284.

[343] *Ibid.*, p. 435.

5

Farmers, Convicts, and Soldiers

Virginians, unlike the New England Puritans, assumed that a heterogeneous population was both socially and economically desirable, and on only one point was there any deviation from this idea. Religious uniformity was always insisted upon, and dissenters from the Anglican Church — whether Papist or Protestant — were made to feel unwelcome and were discriminated against both socially and under the law.[344] In fact, George Brent of Woodstock Plantation in Stafford County was believed to have been the only Roman Catholic living in Virginia in 1681.[345] It must be pointed out, however, in reference to our present concern, that the Brent family of Virginia and the Blount or Bunt family of Maryland and Virginia were both derived from the Italian family of Biondi and that they were both related to the English-Italian family of Boldero.[346]

Thus far, we have assumed that most of those bearing Italian names who came to Virginia came as Englishmen of Italian extraction and were of the Anglican faith. Some, however, may have come to the colony directly from Italy, although it would be impossible to sort out which ones. Also, some of those who came to the colony through an English way-station, may never have been naturalized in England. It is entirely possible that individuals came to the colony from other countries such as France, Germany, or even Spain or Portugal without the benefit of English naturalization. Entirely in keeping with the Virginia attitude toward the reception of foreigners, the Assembly in 1671 adopted its own naturalization law. The preamble to the act is most revealing:

> Whereas nothing can tend more to be advancement of a new plantation
> either to its defence or prosperity, nor nothing add to the glory of a prince
> than [his] being a gratious master of many subjects, nor any way to

---

[344] R.C. Harper, *The Course of the Melting Pot Idea*, p. 45.

[345] Minutes of a Committee of Trade and Plantations, November 26, 1681, *VMHB*, XXVI (February, 1918), 41n.

[346] G.E. Schiavo, *The Italians in America Before the Civil War*, p. 342; *VMHB*, XXVI (January, 1918), 41n. John Boldero of London married Margaret Brent, sister of Edmund Brent of Westmoreland County, Virginia, on September 20, 1675. "Historical and Genealogical Notes", *WMQ* First Series, (April, 1918), 287. *See also*, Lyon G. Tyler, "Washington and his Neighbors", *WMQ*, First Series, IV (July, 1895), 31, 39n. In 1650, a "Mr. Baldero" was ordered to leave Scotland "under pain of death if he return". G.F. Black, *The Surnames of Scotland*, p. 46. Black does not say this "Mr. Baldero" was Scottish not does he suggest that the name here is of Italian origin.

produce these effects than the inviting of people of other nations to reside among us,...*Be it therefore enacted*...that any strangers desiring to make this court the place of their court and residence, may upon application to the grand assembly, and taking the oath of allegiance and supremacy to his majestie [,] be admitted to naturalization.[347]

The Naturalization Act itself proceeded to lay down the principle that all naturalized subjects of the crown should have all rights and privileges of "natural-born Englishmen", the only possible obstacle in the process being the fee of 800 pounds of tobacco to be paid to the Secretary of the Colony and 400 pounds of tobacco to be paid to the clerk.[348]

While the Naturalization Act of 1671 was a general invitation to all foreigners to come to Virginia, the royal governor, Sir William Berkeley, assumed his own positive action toward bringing in foreigners. In this case, however, the immigrants were Italians directly from Italy. Berkeley himself had planted mulberry trees in the hope of producing silk, and in a letter to the Committee of Trade and Plantations, the governor wrote that skilled men should be brought to Virginia from Naples and Sicily to teach the "silkmaker's art". Berkeley was quite optimistic, predicting that "in less than an age, we should make as much silk in a year as England did yearly expend three-score years since".[349]

Although the Virginia records give the names of persons naturalized under the act during the next few years, the individuals are simply listed as "alien", and no country of origin is indicated. At any rate, no obviously Italian names appear in the naturalization records.[350] Even Governor Berkeley's plan found no immediate favor in England, and the mulberry trees were soon forgotten. In 1675, however, a Mr. Ball, British envoy to the Grand Duchy of Tuscany, writing from Leghorn, proposed to the Privy Council that Greeks from Morea be sent to Virginia to escape persecution by the Turks. These "very industrious people", he wrote, could produce "Oil, Wine, Wax, Cotton and Silk". The proposal was laid aside by the Privy Council "as a thing of change".[351] One must wonder why one writing from the Tuscan port proposed sending Greeks rather than Italians.

While Ball's suggestion was officially ignored, the hope of receiving non-English immigrants in Virginia lived on — both in the colony and in England. In 1697, for instance, John Locke, the famous political philosopher, took up the argument,

[347] Hening, *Statutes*, II, 289-290.

[348] *Ibid.*, II, 290.

[349] Governor Sir William Berkeley [to the Committee of Trade and Plantations], January 22, 1671/2, *VMHB*, XX (April, 1912), 126-127. *C.f., VMHB*, XX (January, 1912), 17.

[350] In the first group were John Mulder, Henry Weedick, Christopher Ryault, Henry Fayson Vandoverage, John Mattone, Dominick Theriate, Jeremy Pacquett, Nicholas Cook, Henry Waggamore, and Thomas Harmenson. Hening, *Statutes*, II, 302. *C.f., Ibid.*, II, 308, 339.

[351] Ball to Secretary Joseph Williamson, from Leghorn, May 25, 1675, *VMHB*, XX (July, 1912), 240-241.

writing, and without making any suggestion of country of origin, that:

> by every new foreigner that settles in the English Plantation, the King gains a new Subject without any loss, whereas by every English man settled there he gains a new subject to the Plantation but loses an old Subject for him in England. So...let people of all nations be naturalized, and enjoy equal priviledges, with the other English inhabitants residing there.[352]

By the close of the seventeenth century, indentured servitude had "peaked", as Virginia tobacco planters found chattel slavery to be the more satisfactory form of labor. White "servants" had to be replaced when their time of service expired, while black slaves were the property of the planter for the rest of their lives. Fewer whites were "brought" to Virginia during the eighteenth century, but among those who came were, as we shall see, still a considerable number of persons bearing Italian names. Furthermore, in 1699, the Virginia General Court excluded blacks from the headright and allowed individuals to purchase land at the rate of 5s. per 50 acres.[353]

Perhaps the most significant trend in the white immigration pattern is that while fewer individuals were coming as voluntary indentured servants, more were being sent to Virginia as convicts, a trend which became particularly noticeable after 1718.[354]

In the year 1700, the Virginia Assembly acted on its own to promote foreign immigration when it invited persecuted French Huguenot refugees to settle at Mankintown on the south side of the James River just above the falls. The region was set off as King William Parish of Henrico County. The French immigrants were to be given land by families, and all refugees were to be excused from payment of taxes for seven years.[355] The reliable estimate is that between 700 and 800 men, women, and children came to the settlement during the next three or four years.[356]

Among the French refugees at Mankintown were probably several families of Italian origin, as it is well known that Italian Waldensians had long migrated northward to Switzerland and France, and Italian Protestants had come to England since the days of Queen Elizabeth I. Giovanni Ermenegildo Schiavo has identified such Italian families among the Huguenot refugees in South Carolina as Vallo, Sallari, Svineau, Peronneau, and Prioleau, the latter being traced to the Doge Privli of Venice,[357] and the reasonable conjecture would be

---

[352] Quoted in Michael G. Kammen, ed., "Virginia at the Close of the Seventeenth Century: an Appraisal by James Blair and John Locke", *VMHB*, 74 (April, 1966), 155, 159.

[353] John Kukla, "Introduction" to N.M. Nugent, *Cavaliers and Pioneers*, III, vii-viii.

[354] P.W. Coldham, *English Convicts in Colonial America*, I, x-xi.

[355] Hening, *Statutes*, III, 201.

[356] Robert Beverley, *The History and Present State of Virginia*, (Indianapolis and New York: Bobbs Merrill Company, 1971 ed.), Pp. 146-147.

[357] G.E. Schiavo, *The Italians in America Before the Civil War*, p. 131. *See also*, Arthur Henry Hirsch,

that some of the Huguenot families that came to Virginia were also of Italian extraction.

Without definitely ascribing Italian origins, several Henrico County families might be mentioned as possibilities: Salle,[358] Sabatie,[359] Callio,[360] Mattoone,[361] Bellomy (or Bellomi?),[362] Levia,[363] Capoone,[364] Parranto (or Parento),[365] Farsi, Bilbo, Bingli, Gori, Copei, Scotte,[366] Allegre (Allagre), Buffo, Curzenove, Lucado, Billo, and Pero.[367]

By the beginning of the eighteenth century, there had been, as we have seen, something of a concentration of families of Italian origin on the Eastern Shore and in the counties on the south bank of the James River. Indeed, the portion of Nansemond County in the Cypress Swamp and Sarum Creek region is mentioned in several 1702 land titles as that "commonly called the Banks of Italy", and the same region was indicated on contemporary maps as "Italia".[368] The Rent Roll Census of 1704-1705 lists Christopher Blico with 50 acres and Obedience Cardenscaire with 200 acres in Surry County; James Lupo with 45 acres, Philip Pardoe with 100 acres, Robert Mongo with 400 acres, and Thomas

---

The Huguenots of Colonial South Carolina. Durham: Duke University Press, 1928, Pp. 41, 52ff.

[358] Several members of the Salle family patented land in Henrico County and counties to the west. Land Office Catalog, Virginia State Library.

[359] The will of one Peter Sabatie was probated in Henrico County in 1712. *Virginia Wills and Administrations, 1632-1800*, p. 370.

[360] Joseph Callio, in 1716, patented land specifically indicated as within the territory assigned to the Huguenots. N.M. Nugent, *Cavaliers and Pioneers*, III, 182; Land Office Catalog, Virginia State Library.

[361] In 1715, Anthony Mattoone patented 107 acres in Henrico County, and the folllowing year he patented an additional 58 acres, "It being part of the first 5000 A surveyed for French refugees". Land Office Catalog, Virginia State Library.

[362] John Bellomy was one of sixteen persons brought for headrights in Henrico County 1717. N.M. Nugent, *Cavaliers and Pioneers*, III, 193. In 1756, Elizabeth Bellima patented 133 acres in Sussex County, Land Office Catalog, Virginia State Library.

[363] Peter Levia was one of 11 persons brought for headrights in Henrico County by Anthony Trebue in 1717. *Ibid.*, III, 201.

[364] In 1617, Jacob Copoone patented 34 acres in Henrico County. Land Office Catalog, Virginia State Library. A Gideon Chamboone patented land in the same county in 1716. *Ibid.*

[365] In the list of tithables of King William Parish for 1723 was one Isaac Praenteau, although in subsequent records the spelling became Parranto, Parento, and Porenteaux. Vestry Book of King William Parish, Virginia, 1707-1750, *VMHB*, VII (January, 1905), 241, 250, 252. The spelling here is alternating French and Italian forms.

[366] *Ibid.*, VII, 67, 70.

[367] Register...of the Baptisms Made in the Church of the French Refugees at Mankintown, in R.A. Brock, ed., *Documents Chiefly Unpublished Relating to the Huguenot Emigration to Virginia*, Vol V of *Collections* of the Virginia Historical Society (Richmond: The Virginia Historical Society, 1896), x, xii, 47, 79, 80n., 84, 79, 94, 114, 115; Tithables in King William Parish, *WMQ*, First Series, VIII (July, 1899), 31-32.

[368] Virginia State Land Office, County Abstracts, Nansemond County, April 25, 1702, and July 15, 1717. *C.f.* N.M. Nugent, *Cavaliers and Pioneers*, III, 57, 191. A 1773 map is in Philip Mazzei, *My Life and Wanderings*, Margherita Marchione, ed. (Morristown, NJ, 1980), following p. 202.

Mandue with 200 acres in Isle of Wight County; Isaac Sketto (Schetto?) with 100 acres, Edward Sketto with 200 acres, and Francis Sketto with 100 acres in Nansemond County; John Levima with 510 acres and Morris Velle with 335 acres in Norfolk County; William Grinto with 650 acres in Princess Anne County; James Lingoe with 200 acres and William Lingoe with 300 acres in Accomack County; and Daniel Francisco with 150 acres in Northampton County. For this same year, in Charles City County, Samuel Ele held 652 acres and John Tarendine 150; in King and Queen County, Francis Pomea held 100 acres, Charles Simpio 100, and Arthur Letto 475; and in Gloucester County Isaac Valine held 100 acres. Not to be forgotten are the Taliaferros, who in Essex County held: Francis, 1,300 acres; Charles, 300 acres; and John 2,000. Also in Essex County was the 100-acre holding of Salvator Musco.[369]

It is, of course, to be noted that several of these names appear in the 1704 rent rolls for the first time. Salvator Musco (sometimes spelled Muscoe), for example, was perhaps typical of the enterprising early eighteenth century immigrant. Having both financial capital and social connections,[370] his wife being the sister of Colonel William Beverley,[371] he acquired his first Essex County lands immediately upon his arrival in the colony. Although he is listed as having been "brought" to Virginia to satisfy headright claims of Francis Shelby,[372] he was certainly not an indentured servant. To his original landholding, Musco made several additions,[373] and within two decades he was recognized as one of the larger landholders in Essex County. Evidently he was a man of some education, and he was recognized by his contemporaries as a man of culture and a leading citizen, or as one Virginia historian noted, "a man of Prominence in his county".[374] During his early years in Virginia, Salvator Musco served as Colonel in the Virginia militia. In 1726 he was appointed Justice of the Peace for Essex County, [375] and in 1730 he was appointed Sheriff of the same county. He also represented Essex County in the House of Burgesses in 1736-1738 and in 1740.[376] He died in 1741, and his widow died in 1750.[377]

[369] The list is given in T.J. Wertenbaker, *The Planters of Colonial Virginia*, Pp. 181-233.

[370] In his will, Musco stated that his sister, Mrs. Jane Collingwood "of Great Britain", had left him £400. This bequest, however, came in 1730, but it does indicate that he had relatives of considerable financial means. W.G. Stanard, *Some Emigrants to Virginia*, 2nd ed. (Baltimore: Southern Book Company, 1953), p. 61.

[371] Philip Alexander Bruce, "Mosco, the Indian", *Tyler's Quarterly*, VII (April, 1926), 251-252. One of the great-grandmothers of Colonel William Barnard of Nansemond County was one Cecily Muscote. Byrd Genealogy, *VMHB*, VI (April, 1899), 409.

[372] N.M. Nugent, *Cavaliers and Pioneers*, III, 104.

[373] *Ibid.*, III, 273; Land Office Catalog, Virginia State Library; Virginia State Land Office, County Abstracts, Elizabeth City County.

[374] Virginia Council Journals, 1726-1753, *VMHB*, XXXV (October, 1927), 416n.

[375] The Present State of Virginia of Governor Hugh Drysdale, 1726, in *VMHB*, XVVIII (April, 1940), 144.

[376] P.A. Bruce, "Mosco", p. 252n.   [377] *Virginia Wills and Administrations, 1632-1800*, p. 308.

The Garro family, which probably dates from the same period, is noted only in the record of probated wills, with several changes in spelling in successive generations. The will of William Garro was probated in York County in 1707, that of a second William in Surry County in 1727 (here spelled Garrott), of John Garrott in Amelia County in 1744, and that of Isaac Garrot in Chesterfield in 1775.[378]

In 1712, the first Vivian appears in the Virginia records. The Vivians, it will be remembered, traced their ancestry back to the days of the Roman occupation of Britain. Although members of this family must have been in Virginia for some time before that date, on July 21, 1712, John Vivian was appointed Justice of the Peace for Middlesex County, and the following year he was appointed Sheriff of the same county, with reappointment for several years following. In 1729, Thomas Vivian was appointed Sheriff of King George County.[379]

The Mozingo family, too, can be traced, after a fashion, through their wills. Four generations of Edward Mozingos had wills probated in Richmond County — 1712, 1754, 1783, and 1795.[380]

Still another family was that of Avera. Henry Avera had doubtless come to Virginia in the 1690s as an indentured servant, as his Elizabeth City County estate, settled in 1721, "paid John Stores his account for buying James Avera",[381] who may have been a son. Charles Avera, Henry's brother, operated a sizeable plantation in the 1740s. There were also three other Averas in Elizabeth City County during this period. Certainly to be noted here is that the spelling of Avera became "Avery". Alexander Avera, however, was still using the original spelling of the name as late as 1755, when in that year he patented 267 acres "in the Upper part of Nansemond County".[382] Later families which can be traced through probated wills were the Sabastines (spelling alternating with Sebastian) between 1735 and 1773 in King George, Lancaster, Fairfax, and Stafford Counties,[383] and the Cuttilos of Lunenburg County between 1755 and 1790.[384]

One of the most intriguing figures in eighteenth-century Virginia history was the Reverend John Garzia, who in 1720 became rector of Northfarnham Parish in Richmond County on the neck between the Potomac and Rappahannock Rivers. Although one Virginia ecclesiastical historian has speculated that Garzia was Spanish,[385] the name is always given in the Italian form, and there is little

---

[378] Ibid., p. 165.

[379] Executive Journals of the Council of Colonial Virginia, III, 318, 338, 371, 500; IV, 200.

[380] Virginia Wills and Administrations, p. 301.

[381] Blanche Adams Chapman, Wills and Administrations of Elizabeth City County, Virginia, 1688-1800 (Baltimore: Genealogical Publishing Co., 1980), p.9.

[382] Hening, Statutes, VI, 508-509. In 1782 Hanna Avera was listed as a property-holder in Elizabeth City County. B.A. Chapman, Wills and Administrations of Elizabeth City County, Virginia, 1688-1800, p. 147.

[383] Virginia Wills and Administrations, 1632-1800, Pp. 370, 378.   [384] Ibid., p. 109.

[385] George MacLaren Brydon, Virginia's Mother Church and the Political Conditions Under Which it Grew, 2 vols. (Richmond: Virginia Historical Society, and Philadelphia: Church Historical Society, 1947-

doubt that he was of Italian origin or that he had once been a Roman Catholic priest. Whatever his origin, George Whitfield, the famous English evangelist, wrote in 1741 to the Bishop of Oxford that Garzia could scarcely speak English.[386]

John and Mary Garzia had four children, each baptized in Northfarnham Parish: Katherine (1720), Jane (1721), Anne (1725), and John (1731).[387] Whatever may have been Garzia's linguistic limitations, they were most certainly offset by his religious zeal. Perhaps somewhat unusual among Virginia Anglican clergy of the time, Garzia was especially concerned for the spiritual needs of the blacks within the parish, having at one time 354 blacks listed on the parish register.[388] In 1735, Garzia left Virginia for a parish in North Carolina, where he died in 1744 as the result of a fall from a horse.[389]

Another most interesting person of the period was Dr. John DeSequeyra, who has frequently, albeit erroneously, been identified as Italian,[390] and hence mention must be made of him here. Actually, DeSequeyra (born in London in 1712) came from a famous family of Portuguese, Jewish physicians and took his medical degree from the University of Leiden in 1739. In 1745, he came to Virginia and began his medical practice in or near Williamsburg, where he enjoyed a high reputation for his medical skills. Thomas Jefferson credited him with introducing the tomato as an edible plant. When the Virginia Hospital for the Insane, the first institution of its kind in what is now the United States, opened in 1773, DeSequeyra was appointed the Hospital's official physician. He died in 1795.[391]

Just as had been the case during the seventeenth century, throughout the eighteenth century, or until the American Revolution, the Virginia records carry the names of persons with Italian origin who merited a brief official mention and then disappeared. Although these individuals may have had little or no impact

1952), I, 235. In the Spanish form, "Garcia" is a place name deriving from the Spanish city Garcia. J.N. Hook.

[386] Edward Lewis Goodwin, The Colonial Church in Virginia (Milwaukee: Morehouse Publishing Co., 1927), p. 271.

[387] Register of North Farnham Parish, 1663-1814, and Lunenburg Parish, 1783-1806, Richmond County, Virginia, Compiled by George Harrison Sanford King (Fredericksburg: Published by the Compiler, 1966), p. 66.

[388] Joan R. Gundersen, "The Non-Institutional Church: The Religious Role of Women in Eighteenth-Century Virginia", Historical Magazine of the Protestant Episcopal Church, LI (December, 1982), 325.

[389] A List of Counties, Parishes, and Present Ministers of Virginia, March 25, 1735, VMHB, 58 (October, 1950), 407; E.L. Goodwin, The Colonial Church in Virginia, p. 271.

[390] E.G. Schiavo, The Italians in America Before the Civil War, p. 135. He was identified by Lyon Gardiner Tyler as "probably one of the Educated Italians, who came with Philip Mazzei to this country". Williamsburg, The Old Colonial Capital (Richmond: Whittet and Schepperson, 1907), p. 244n.

[391] Wyndham B. Blanton, Medicine in Virginia in the Seventeenth Century (Richmond: William Byrd Press, 1930), p. 288; Harold B. Gell, "Dr. De Sequezra's Diseases of Virginia", VMHB, 86 (July, 1978), 294; Letter of E. Randolph Braxton to "Notes and Queries", VMHB, XLI (January, 1933), 73.

upon the society of which they were a part, our interest in the Italian presence demands that they be at least mentioned.

Even though indentured servants had given way to chattel slavery as the basic labor system, white "servants" continued to come to Virginia, although in steadily decreasing numbers. Yet among these humble folk were still those of apparently Italian origin, and among those who entered servitude of their own choice were Thomas Amore (brought to King William County in 1702),[392] Mary Delivcore (brought to James City County in 1702),[393] John Battice (to Prince George County in 1705),[394] Elizabeth Trappo (to King and Queen County in 1705),[395] *Abraham Debeta* (to Isle of Wight County in 1713),[396] and John Meccola (to King William County in 1714).[397]

For the same century, there is, alas, an even larger list of those sentenced to Virginia as punishment for crimes. Those who were specifically sentenced to serve their time in Virginia were William Beddo (1727),[398] Dominique Pillo (Pulla) (1731),[399] Elizabeth Teno (1734),[400] and Mary Bunco (alias Mary Smith) (1736)[401]. Obadiah Fancia was ordered transported to in 1730 and landed in Annapolis, Maryland, although he may have gone to Virginia later.[402] Others who were sentenced to "transportation", although their destination is not given in the English court record, and may have come to Virginia, were Richard Fardo (1718),[403] John Carbello (1727),[404] Jacob Cordosa (1743),[405] James Jacomo (1748),[406] Joseph Senturelli (1750),[407] Margaret Bruenna (1758),[408] Margaret Tuniola (1761),[409] Joseph Pisano (1769),[410] William Niccoli (1771),[411] and Thomas Peto (1774).[412] As Virginia and Maryland were the presumed "dumping grounds" for convicts after 1718,[413] it may be assumed that at least some of these transported felons came to Virginia.

Not all of those with names indicative of Italian origins came as servants or felons, and the record is replete with names which are found in neither headright lists or shiplists. There were evidently persons who came to the colony at their own expense and, except for a brief glimpse in one sort of official record or another, would seem to have been otherwise unnoticed.

Here the land records reveal much. In 1710, Samuel Duchiminia patented 440 acres of escheated land in Westmoreland County, and the following year

---

[392] N.M. Nugent, *Cavaliers and Pioneers*, III, 66. Here, as in the preceding chapter, the county in which the headright was given is assumed, tentatively, to be that in which the person "brought in" was settled.

[393] *Ibid.*, III, 63.   [394] *Ibid.*, III, 104.   [395] *Ibid.*, III, 99.   [396] *Ibid.*, III, 133.   [397] *Ibid.*, III, 144.

[398] Peter Wilson Coldham, *English Convicts in Colonial America*, 2 vols. (New Orleans: Polyanthos, 1974-1976), I, 20.

[399] *Ibid.*, II, 117.   [400] *Ibid.*, I, 262. She arrived in Virginia in December, 1734, on the *Caesar*.

[401] *Ibid.*, I, 246.   [402] *Ibid.*, II, 52.   [403] *Ibid.*, II, 52.   [404] *Ibid.*, I, 47.   [405] *Ibid.*, I, 64.

[406] *Ibid.*, I, 144.   [407] *Ibid.*, II, 132.   [408] *Ibid.*, II, 27.   [409] *Ibid.*, I, 270.   [410] *Ibid.*, I, 211.

[411] *Ibid.*, I, 196.   [412] *Ibid.*, I, 116.   [413] *Ibid.*, I, x.

he patented 202 acres in Stafford County.[414] In a similar case, John Blinco in 1722 presented a petition "to dock entailed lands in Northumberland" County.[415] In 1734, John Stita (assuming that this is not a clerk's error in transcribing the name "Stith") purchased a tract of land in Orange County.[416] William Connico patented several small tracts in Spotsylvania County in 1725 and 1726.[417] John Partlo was already a resident of Caroline County when in 1729 he patented 200 acres in St. Margaret's Parish, "about 200 yards above his home".[418] Robert Faldo apparently held land in Caroline County, as in 1730 he became involved in a title suit involving both Ralph Wormley and William Taliaferro.[419] Others who patented land were John Tomasone (150 acres in Spotsylvania County, 1731),[420] Marquis Calmenze (108 acres in Stafford County, 1741),[421] Caleb Eliste (190 acres in Surry County, 1743),[422] John Rippeto (120 acres in Louisa County in 1768 and 83 acres in Albemarle County in 1771),[423] and Conrad Debo (300 acres in Frederick County, 1770).[424] It may be noted here that many of these landholdings were in the newer, back-woods counties.

Persons whose names appear as landholders (but without indication of the size of their landholdings) were Barbara Dinto (a landholder in Goochland County in the early 1730s),[425] James Milo (one of many signers from the "back parts of Virginia" asking Governor William Gooch for more adequate defense),[426] Thomas Gimbo (Spotsylvania County in the early 1760s),[427] Isaac Tolverine (listed as holding one slave in Princess Anne County in 1771),[428] Anthony

---

[414] Index: Northern Neck Grants and Surveys, Virginia State Library. Escheated lands had, for one reason or another, reverted to the colony government under Virginia law and may have been "improved" lands. Estates of executed felons, for example, reverted to the colony, and the lands mentioned here may have "reverted" under such circumstances.

[415] Notes from the Journal of the House of Burgesses, 1712-1726, WMQ, First Series, XXI (April, 1913), 254. Virginia's entail laws forbade the division of landed property during one's lifetime. Although the law was not strictly enforced, there were occasions when an attempted division was thwarted and the property in question put up to public sale.

[416] The Friend Family Notes by J.C. Earley from Henrico County Records and Chesterfield County Records, compiled by Charles E. Friend, WMQ, Second Series, XI (April, 1931), 149.

[417] Land Office Catalog, Virginia State Library; N.M. Nugent, Cavaliers and Pioneers, III, 292, 310-311.

[418] Land Office Catalog, Virginia State Library, N.M. Nugent, Cavaliers and Pioneers, III, 362.

[419] Lewis Beckner, "Caroline County Survey Book", WMQ, First Series (January, 1911), 169.

[420] Land Office Catalog, Virginia State Library.

[421] Index: Northern Neck Grants and Surveys, Virginia State Library.

[422] Land Office Catalog, Virginia State Library.   [423] Ibid.

[424] Index: Northern Neck Grants and Surveys, Virginia State Library.

[425] N.M. Nugent, Cavaliers and Pioneers, III, 495.

[426] Calender of Virginia State Papers, 1652-1781 (Richmond: Superintendent of Public Printing, 1875), p. 235.

[427] Virginia Wills and Administrations, 1632-1800, p. 171.

[428] Lower Norfolk County Antiquary, III (1899), 6.

Fullitone (mentioned as a landholder in Lunenburg County in 1775),[429] and Abraham Golindo (who held 44 acres in Princess Anne County in 1775).[430]

Those whose names appear in the probate records as having made wills or having held sufficient personal property to warrant an inventory of his or her estate were John Chimino (Goochland County, 1736),[431] Thomas Carrico (Stafford County, 1798),[432] Joseph Dimmillo (DiMillo?) (Essex County, 1749),[433] Hugh Divinney (sic) Frederick County, 1759), and Cornelius Divinia (1790),[434] William Angello, Sr., (Cumberland County, 1769),[435] and Ezekiel Vete (Frederick County, 1773).[436] Mentioned in wills as beneficiaries or as witnesses were Mary Murelle (witness, Isle of Wight County, 1730),[437] Benjamin Fernando (one of the "back counties", 1759),[438] Thomas Pauleto (legatee, Louisa County, 1767 or 1768).[439] From the legal records it is learned that in 1723, William Faldo, apparently a merchant or shipowner, brought suit against William Livingston, the operator of the theater at Williamsburg.[440] According to the marriage records, Alexander Howard married Joana Tripolo (Spotsylvania County, 1727),[441] William Jones married Mary Dedeo in 1760, Thomas Weldon married Ruth Pantoli in 1753, William Prata married Courtney Edmunds in 1755, and William S. Lane married Courtney Prato in 1763, all in Norfolk County.[442] The baptismal records of Albemarle Parish, Surry County, record that of William, son of John and Mary Mattla, on October 4, 1741.[443] A final mention on this ecclesiastical note is that Daniel Fristo achieved a bit of notoriety when in the early 1770s, he became a spokesman for the highly unpopular Baptist movement.[444]

Christopher Francisco and his sons also figured prominently in back-country Virginia. Francisco was of Italian origin and came to Lancaster County, Pennsylvania, via Switzerland some time before 1710. Francisco joined the

[429] *Edward Pleasants Valentine Papers*, II, 675.

[430] *Lower Norfolk County Antiquary*, III (1899), 3.

[431] *Virginia Wills and Administrations, 1632-1800*, p. 81.

[432] *Ibid.*, p. 72.   [433] *Ibid.*, p. 121.   [434] *Ibid.*, p. 122.   [435] *Ibid.*, p. 10.   [436] *Ibid.*, p. 435.

[437] B.A. Chapman, *Wills and Administrations of Isle of Wight County, 1642-1800*, II, 96.

[438] Abstracts of Pine Grove [Record] Book, *WMQ*, Second Series, XI (July, 1948), 367.

[439] *Edward Pleasants Valentine Papers*, III, 1676.

[440] Robert H. Land, "The First Williamsburg Theater", *WMQ*, Third Series, V, (July, 1948), 367.

[441] Early Spotsylvania Marriage Licenses, *VMHB*, IV (October, 1896), 198.

[442] Mrs. Russell S. Barrett, Comp. "Marriage Bonds of Norfolk County", *WMQ*, Second Series, VIII (April, 1928), 100-104. The Lane-Prata marriage was performed in St. Paul's Church, Norfolk. *Lower Norfolk County Antiquary*, IV (1902), 19.

[443] *Register of Albemarle Parish, Surry and Sussex Counties*, edited by Gertrude R.B. Richards (Richmond: Colonial Dames of America in the Commonwealth of Virginia, 1958), p. 76.

[444] Rhys Isaac, "Evangelical Revolt: The Nature of the Baptists' Challenge to the Traditional Order in Virginia, 1765 to 1775", *WMQ*, Third Series, XXXI (July, 1974), 355.

southward movement of Pennsylvania Germans into the Shenandoah Valley, where he was one of the first permanent settlers. By the time of his death in 1765, he had acquired some 4,000 acres in Augusta County. One of Francisco's daughters married Henry Hill, a large landholder in the Valley, and his two sons, Christopher, Junior, and Ludovick, were influential in Shenandoah Valley affairs. During the French and Indian War, Ludovick served as a Captain of Foot in the Augusta County Militia.[445]

The American Revolution mobilized a considerable portion of the white, adult, male Virginia population, and again, from the lists available, it can be learned that Virginians of Italian extraction served in both the Continental Army and the Virginia Militia in admirable proportion to the total population.

Many of their names have already been mentioned or will be given in our following chapter, but to the already impressive list must be added the names of Cosmo Medici, a resident of Virginia who entered a North Carolina regiment with rank of captain,[446] James Romindo,[447] Francesco Monte,[448] Samuel Edo,[449] Ferdinando Firrizzi, who was present with General Washington at the surrender of Lord Cornwallis at Yorktown,[450] Stephen Verde, private,[451] and those who served under General George Rogers Clark in the Illinois Country: Sergeant Francis Rubido, and privates J.B. deCoste, Francis Lofaro, James Rubido, and Lewis and Michael Campo.[452]

---

[445] Land Office Catalog, Virginia State Library; Journal of the Council of Virginia in Executive Session, 1757-1763; *VMHB*, XIV (October, 1906), 123n.; Pedigree of a Representative Virginia Planter [Virginia Pedigree of Digges] *WMQ*, First Series, I (January, 1893), 150; J.A. Waddell, *Annals of Augusta County*, p. 92.

[446] G.E. Schiavo, *The Italians in America Before the Civil War*, Pp. 267-268; M.A. Musmanno, *The Story of the Italians in America*, p. 9.

[447] Ruby Altizer Roberts, "Montgomery County's Revolutionary Heritage", *VMHB*, XVVI (October, 1938), 340.

[448] M.A. Musmanno, *The Story of the Italians in America*, p. 9.

[449] *WMQ*, First Series VI (January, 1898), 190.

[450] M.A. Musmanno, *The Story of the Italians in America*, p. 9.

[451] Payroll for a detachment of Different Regiments on their march to Head Quarters Under Command of Captain Burnley and Lieut. Sam'l. Gill, April 14th, 1778, *VMHB* I, (October, 1883), 205-206.

[452] "The Illinois Regiment and the Northwest Territory", *VMHB*, I (October, 1893), 134.

6

The Intellectuals

Although the Italian physical presence was certainly impressive during the first 150 years of Virginia history, the cultural impact was slight. Most of those of Italian extraction had come to the colony via England, and the vast majority of them seem to have been, culturally, totally anglicized by the time they reached Virginia. Furthermore, those who had brief stop-overs in England were probably from the lower classes and would hardly have been in a position to carry much "cultural baggage" with them. Even at this early date, the "melting pot" was busily boiling down the various ethnic components of colonial America to something of a least-common-denominator culture, which, with each succeeding generation, diminished the most obvious cultural characteristics of the ethnic groups in favor of a basically English transplant in which non-English elements found little place.

Virginians welcomed non-English people, and non-English people accepted gladly Virginia's invitation to migrate. Even in Italy, there were those who at least gave thought to migration, although few of them took the step. This last item is odd, especially in view of the general lack of social and economic opportunity available to the inhabitants of the Italian states during the seventeenth and eighteenth centuries. America was a faraway land, far beyond what most Italians would have found within their hopes.

Yet, America was well known to educated, upper-class Italians. Benjamin Franklin, for example, was read in Italy by those who cared to learn of the Philadelphian's latest experiments in electricity.[453] In 1763, two significant Italian translations of English books appeared in Italy. A publisher in Leghorn printed the *American Gazetteer*, and a printing house in Venice issued Edmund Burke's *An Account of the European Settlements in America*. Burke's translator noted in a preface that of all European people, the Italians were the only ones with no colonies to which they could migrate. He urged, therefore, that Italians go to America where, he declared, the British government would gladly provide land.[454] One can only wonder what the effect might have been, had the idea been advanced on a large scale a century earlier.

---

[453] Antonio Pace, *Benjamin Franklin and Italy* (Philadelphia: The American Philosophical Society, 1958), *passim*, especially Chapter I.

[454] Alexander De Conde, *Half Bitter, Half Sweet* (New York: Charles Scribner's Sons, 1971), p. 3.

Seventeenth-century Virginia planters, with their cultural pattern being set in an imitation of the life-style of the English country gentry, seem to have been little influenced by Italian cultural developments. The Latin classics were respected, even venerated, but the vast body of Italian literature, music, sculpture, painting, and architecture was largely ignored. Although the writings of the sixteenth-century Italian architect Andrea Palladia had been available in English since 1663, the Palladian style did not become influential before the Revolution.[455]

The rural nature of Virginia society, too, precluded any significant Italian influence upon Virginia music. Lacking an urban center, and remembering that even Williamsburg had a population of less than 2,000 on the eve of the Revolution, the elaborate concerts which were so much a fact of life of Philadelphia, New York, and Charleston, could hardly have been expected in a colony whose centers of activity were small courthouse towns. This was found to have been painfully true by Francis Alberti who came from Italy to Williamsburg in the late 1760s, hoping to make a living as a violinist. Although he enjoyed no success as a concert artist, he was able to support himself by giving lessons. Thomas Jefferson was among Alberti's pupils, and Jefferson's wife took lessons on the harpsichord. During the year 1771, Alberti spent some time at Monticello giving music lessons to various members of the Jefferson family. In 1774, Alberti joined Thomas Jefferson, Anderson Bryan and Francis Eppes in endorsing the "Nonimportation Association" of the Continental Congress,[456] although he seems to have otherwise shunned a public civic life.

Although music in concert was not a normal part of seventeenth or eighteenth century Virginia life, there were rare examples of individuals who at least had some superficial acquaintance with Italian music scores and Italian-language books. For example, the inventory of the estate of William Borcus of Lancaster County, probated in 1655, included books in Latin, Spanish, and Italian,[457] although whether he could read them is another matter. Also, the inventory of the estate of Cuthbert Ogle, a bookseller, who died in Williamsburg in 1755, listed a large number of music books and collections of Italian songs.[458]

By the mid-eighteenth century, Virginia had made her first direct commercial contacts with Italy, as in 1752, a sailing vessel of 120 tons cleared the port of Hampton for Genoa.[459] Nothing is known of the cargo or even whether there

---

[455] Louis B. Wright, *The Cultural Life of the American Colonies, 1607-1763* (New York: Harper and Brothers, 1957), p. 200.

[456] Dumas Malone, *Jefferson the Virginian* (Boston: Little, Brown and Co., 1948); Pp. 159, 191; *Papers of Thomas Jefferson*, Boyd, *et al.*, eds., I, 154. Alberti died in 1785, James Currie to Thomas Jefferson, August 5, 1785, *Papers of Thomas Jefferson*, Boyd, ed., VIII (Princeton University Press, 1950) I, 156-159.

[457] P.A. Bruce, *Institutional History of Virginia in the Seventeenth Century*, I, 423-424.

[458] *WMQ*, First Series, III (October, 1894), 251-252.

[459] Francis Carroll Huntley, "The Seaborne Trade of Virginia in the Mid-Eighteenth Century: Port Hampton", *VMHB*, 59 (July, 1951), 303.

was a return voyage. It is well known, however, as we shall see, that there was already an extensive market, even in Virginia, for Italian food products.

Also, by the mid-eighteenth century the "Grand Tour" had become popular among colonials who would afford to educate their sons in Europe. Young men who had completed their studies at Oxford, Cambridge, Edinburgh, or the Inns of Court in London spent a year or two in Italy, France, Germany, and the Low Countries as a capstone to their education. There were others who made the Grand Tour independently of academic study in Europe. In 1760, for example, the son of William Allen, Chief Judge of Pennsylvania, sent his son, accompanied by the young painter, Benjamin West, to Leghorn on a vessel carrying a cargo of wheat and flour. West remained in Italy for four years, copying the old masters, becoming something of a favorite in Rome, and being elected to the Academies of Parma, Florence, and Bologna.[460] In 1762, at the age of 21, Henry Benbridge of Philadelphia went to Rome to study art. In 1768, he was commissioned by James Boswell to go to Corsica to paint a full-length portrait of Pasquale Paoli, the Corsican revolutionary who had captured the imagination of both Englishmen and colonials. Upon his return to America, Benbridge became a popular portrait artist in both Virginia and South Carolina.[461]

The already-mentioned Cosmo Medici (deMedici) was a shadowy figure in the decade before the outbreak of the Revolution. Medici was a popular portrait painter working in Virginia in the 1770s, but there is some question as to his identity, or confusion with one who assumed the same name. Some art historians believe that his real name was Cosmo Alexander, a Scotsman who had previously worked in New York and New Jersey as early as 1768, and that he was one of the teachers of Gilbert Stuart.[462] There are others, however, who insist that the southern Medici was indeed an authentic Medici who had come to America to seek fame and fortune.[463]

Thomas Jefferson once noted that although early in life he had taught himself to read Italian, and he could read the language with proficiency, he had never heard it spoken before 1773.[464] One would hardly doubt Jefferson's word, but certainly he was a close friend of Robert Bolling (1738-1775) of Henrico, who, after being educated in England, returned to Virginia in 1756, and,

[460] A. De Conde, *Half Bitter, Half Sweet*, Pp. 18-19.

[461] *Ibid.,* p. 21.

[462] George C. Groce and David H. Wallace, *The New York Historical Society's Dictionary of Artists in America, 1564-1860* (New Haven and London: Yale University Press, 1957), Pp. 4, 437.

[463] G.E. Schiavo, *The Italians in America Before the Civil War*, Pp. 267-269; Mantle Fielding, *Dictionary of American Painters, Sculptors, and Engravers* (Cambridge: William Young and Co., 1968); *VMHB*, XXXIX (January, 1931), 93; Angelo Flavio Guidi, "Washington and the Italians", in Richard C. Garlick, Jr., ed., *Italy and the Italians in Washington's Time* (New York: Italian Publishers, 1933), p. 51n.

[464] Benjamin Franklin also taught himself to read Italian. A. Pace, *Benjamin Franklin and Italy*, p. 1; Franklin, *Autobiography*, various editions, Part Three; G.E. Schiavo, *The Italians in America Before the Civil War*, p. 259.

according to John Randolph of Roanoke, "wrote equally well in Latin, French, and Italian". Bolling wrote several articles on "the cultivation of the grape in Virginia" for the *Virginia Gazette* and wrote at least one piece in Italian for Volume II of the *Columbian Magazine*.[465] It would be hard to understand how one so proficient in writing the language would have been unable to speak it. And, what about Jefferson's friend, Francis Alberti? James Madison could also read Italian in the pre-Revolutionary period, but there is no indication that he could speak it then.[466]

All of this changed in 1773 with the arrival in Williamsburg of Filippo Mazzei. After this, Virginia would never be quite the same. Mazzei was born in 1730 at Poggio a Caiano in Tuscany, studied medicine at the University of Florence, and left the university without taking a degree just one step ahead of the Inquisition. He practiced medicine in Smyrna, Turkey, and in 1755 went to London as personal agent of Grand Duke Leopold I of Tuscany, with whom his friendship was on a first-name basis.

While in London, Mazzei opened a small retail shop specializing in imported foods. The business was operated as Martini and Company, in partnership with an Italian named Joseph Martini, although for some reason Mazzei in his Memoirs always called him Mr. Martin.[467]

Mazzei's interest in America was first aroused by Benjamin Franklin, whom he had met in London because of his curiosity regarding the Franklin stove. Franklin introduced Mazzei to other Americans, and the Italian became particularly attracted to Virginia through Thomas Adams, a Virginian friend of Thomas Jefferson, and a certain Mr. Norton, a London merchant who was married to a Virginian. Each Christmas, Norton invited London's Virginia colony to dinner and always included Mazzei in the group. Adams and Norton helped Mazzei develop a rather extensive trade with America, and particularly with Virginia, shipping "oil, wine, farinacious foods [pasta], Parmesean cheese, small sausages, and anchovies, [all of which] was in demand in America".

Although there was always the commercial interest, late in his life, and long after the American Revolution, Mazzei insisted that the final consideration in his going to America was the prospect of a rebellion by the colonies and his desire to have a part in freeing the colonies of despotism. Franklin and Adams were particularly encouraging, proposing that Mazzei go to Virginia and set himself up "in the vineyard business".

[465] *VMHB*, XXII (July, 1914), 332. Bolling and Jefferson were both signers at the Virginia Non-importation Resolutions of 1769. *The Papers of Thomas Jefferson*, Boyd, ed., I, 30.

[466] G.E Schiavo, *The Italians in America Before the Civil War*, p. 264.

[467] Philip Mazzei, *Memoirs of the Life and Peregrinations of the Florentine, Philip Mazzei, 1730-1816*, translated by Howard R. Marraro (New York: Columbia University Press, 1942), 165. Most of the Mazzei biographical material is taken from the *Memoirs*, Pp. 165ff. A more recent translation is *Philip Mazzei: My Life and Wanderings*, M.S. Eugene Scalia, Margherita Marchione, ed., (Morristown, NJ: American Institute of Italian Studies, 1980).

Following this suggestion, in the spring of 1773, Mazzei wound up his affairs in London and returned to Tuscany to recruit "peasants" to care for the vines he intended to plant. Here he turned to his old friend, the Grand Duke, asking permission to take ten farmers to America. Of those enlisted in the project, one was age 40, and three others were between 18 and 30. The original contingent included one Genoese farmer, two men from Lucca, one of whom was married and had a small child, and a young tailor from Piedmont to take care of the workmen's clothes and serve as Mazzei's house steward.

While gathering his workmen, Mazzei was approached by fifteen-year-old Giovanni Fabbroni, who expressed a desire to go to Virginia. Mazzei was much impressed by the young man and wrote to Thomas Jefferson that the Sage of Monticello would "greatly enjoy the company of a cultivated young Tuscan". The plan misfired, however, as Mazzei had brought the talented young man to the attention of the Grand Duke, who took Fabbroni into his own employ and later made him his principal minister.

Just as the Mazzei party was about to sail, the "peasants" fell victim to a rumor that in America meteors fell with such frequency that it was unsafe to work in the fields. When several of the "peasants" refused to leave, Mazzei had to recruit others. One of these was Vincenzo Rossi, a twenty-year-old farmhand whom Mazzei designated as foreman.

On September 2, 1773, Mazzei's somewhat reconstituted party sailed from Leghorn. On shipboard were Rossi, three farmers from Lucca and Genoa, the tailor, Mrs. Martini, by now the widow of Mazzei's late business partner, and Mrs. Martini's twelve-year-old daughter. The widow and daughter had become Mazzei's charge when Mazzei promised Martini on the latter's deathbed that he would take the two females into his care. Incidentally, several other Italians came to Virginia on a later sailing, and of those ultimately in Mazzei's employ there were probably as many as fourteen.[468]

The Mazzei band arrived in Virginia late in November, 1773, and was greeted in Williamsburg, the Assembly then being in session, by George Washington, Thomas Jefferson, George Wythe, and Mazzei's old London friend, Thomas Adams.

Through the good offices of Adams, the Assembly voted Mazzei 5,000 acres upon which he was to operate a sort of experimental farm in the hope of introducing European vines and vegetables not yet known in America. Mazzei declined the grant and purchased a smaller tract which adjoined that of Jefferson. Mazzei named the farm "Colle". As to the financial arrangement, an elaborate plan was worked out by Jefferson and Mazzei whereby was formed a "Company or Partnership for the Purpose of raising and making Wine, Oil, agruminious Plants and Silk". Shares were sold at £50 sterling each, and

---

[468] Michael A. Musmanno, *The Story of the Italians in America* (Garden City, NY: Doubleday and Co., 1965), p. 11.

among the 35 shareholders were Lord Dunmore, the Royal Governor, with 4 shares, Thomas Adams, George Washington, and Thomas Jefferson with one each, and Mazzei with four.[469]

Mazzei soon became recognized as a man of distinction. Colle was put into active operation in the spring of 1774, and planters from even great distances came to see the Italian farmers at work. Mazzei was advised by this neighbor, Francis Eppes, Jefferson's brother-in-law, that it would be proper for him to marry Mrs. Martini, especially since her daughter was approaching marriageable age, there should be no hint of scandal on the part of the mother. Mazzei and Mrs. Martini were soon married by a justice of the peace, as Mazzei later told this story, but more likely by a priest of the Church of England.

Mazzei's next step was to be naturalized under Virginia law, never having become an English subject during his residence in England. In the summer of 1774 he was elected to the Vestry of St. Anne's Parish of Albemarle County, although in his later years in Europe, not wishing to admit his Anglican affiliation, he wrote that he had been elected to the "Committee to look after the poor". The white lie was not completely white, as the Parish vestries did indeed carry out the workings of the Virginia poor laws, nor was it necessary to have been a communicant to have served on a vestry.

As the colonial break with Mother Britain approached, Mazzei took a firm stand in favor of colonial rights. Late in 1774, he was elected to the Virginia Committee of Correspondence, and soon he was writing, under the name of "Furioso", in the *Virginia Gazette*. Addressing the readers as "dear fellow citizens", Mazzei (Furioso) asserted "that men are by nature equally free and independent" and that "a truly republican form of government cannot exist except where all men...are perfectly equal in their natural rights".[470] The influence of these ideas upon Thomas Jefferson and ultimately the Declaration of Independence is obvious.

After war had actually broken out at the Battles of Lexington and Concord in April, 1775, the rumor spread through Virginia that a British fleet was about to attack Hampton. Mazzei and Jefferson quickly joined an "Independent Company" of militia being raised in Albemarle County to march to Hampton's defense. Charles Lewis was elected Captain, and Mazzei declined an informal commission as Lieutenant "on the grounds of lack of ability". The "company" was soon joined by Vincenzo Rossi and Carlo Bellini, Mazzei's friend about whom we will learn more later.

The volunteers marched bravely toward Hampton, soon to learn that no British attack was planned. Before the company was disbanded, however, it was lined up to hear a speech by Patrick Henry, who a year later would be elected

---

[469] Plan of Philip Mazzei's Agricultural Company, *The Papers of Thomas Jefferson*, Boyd, ed., I, 156-159.

[470] The text of these "letters" is readily available in Anthony F. LoGotto, *The Italians in America: 1492-1972* (Dobbs Ferry, NY: Oceana Publications, 1972), p. 39.

governor of Virginia. As Mazzei later recalled the incident, Henry addressed himself particularly to the three Tuscans. Rossi, who understood hardly a word of English, found Mazzei an excellent simultaneous translator, and, as Mazzei recounted the incident, he "read in his [Rossi's] eloquent face that in that moment he would not have exchanged places with any great lord".

From political philosophy, Mazzei's interests soon turned to religion, joining Thomas Jefferson in working for disestablishment of the Church of England in Virginia. Mazzei's own religious ideas were well known, and although he has frequently been described as something of a free-thinker, he was basically a religious man. Although a Roman Catholic by birth, he had once been a near victim of the Inquisition, but his attitude toward the Church of Rome was one of anti-clericalism rather than one of anti-Romanism. Certainly he had an affection for the Anglican Church, which he found sufficiently Catholic to revere. It was his experience of having lived his entire life in places where a particular religion was "established" — Tuscany, Turkey, England, and Virginia — that caused him to undertake a sort of one-man crusade to place Christians of all denominations on an equal footing in Virginia.

Disestablishment became a favorite topic of conversation, and he never missed an opportunity to present his views at any sort of public gathering. Each Sunday he visited churches of all persuasions, where, following the sermon, he asked for, and received, even in Anglican parish churches, permission to state his case to the congregation. On November 9, 1776, Mazzei was one of 171 signers, his name was number six, describing themselves as "Dissenters from the Church of England", requesting that liberty be granted to all denominations of Christians.[471] A year later, Mazzei joined some 200 others in taking the oath revoking allegiance to King George III both as temporal ruler and head of the Church of England.[472] Also in 1777, Mazzei pledged 16s. 8d. (compared with Jefferson's £6) toward the support of what seems to have been a German Reformed Church in Charlottesville.[473]

Colle had flourished for a while, and Mazzei's horticultural efforts resulted in the introduction of new strains of flowers, fruits, and vegetables and, consequently, new elements in the American diet. Jefferson was so impressed by Mazzei's skills and that of his co-workers that he proposed an expanded immigration from Italy.[474] Mazzei took up the idea and urged his "peasants" to write to friends in Italy urging them to come to Virginia.[475]

---

[471] *Papers of Thomas Jefferson*, Boyd, ed., I, 586-588; *VMHB*, XVIII (July, 1910), 258. One Micajoh Via also signed the petition.

[472] Oath of Allegiance Signed by Citizens of Albemarle County, *Papers of Thomas Jefferson*, Boyd, ed., II, 129.

[473] *Papers of Thomas Jefferson*, Boyd ed., II, 7, 8n.

[474] A.F. Lo Gotto, *The Italians in America*, p. 4.

[475] Henry M. Ward and Harold E. Greer, Jr., *Richmond During the Revolution, 1775-1783* (Charlottesville: University of Virginia Press, 1977), p. 106, describes the building as "modest". There is a conjectural

The operation at Colle collapsed in 1778, when the Continental Congress requisitioned the farm, with its modest dwelling, as a place of detention for Baron Riedesel, the German mercenary general who had been captured at the Battle of Saratoga. All but one of Mazzei's men chose to remain at Colle — temporarily at least — and the General tried, albeit without much success, to continue the operation of a working farm. In 1779, things at Colle went from bad to worse, when Governor Patrick Henry sent Mazzei on a diplomatic mission to the Grand Duchy of Tuscany. The Duke was cordial enough when Mazzei arrived in Florence, but the Virginia diplomat was unable to persuade his old friend to offer any financial assistance for Virginia. Further, Benjamin Franklin, the Minister Plenipotentiary of the Continental Congress in France, sabotaged Mazzei's efforts, and the mission was a total failure.

Although Mazzei could write later that he had left his men "all employed", they were actually left to fend for themselves. Jefferson became something of a patron of the Italian farmers, and for a while at least several of them lived at Monticello. Isaac Jefferson, one of Thomas Jefferson's slaves was much intrigued with the Italians, and in a memoir dictated long after the events recounted, he described life at Monticello. There was, he said, "a tailor named Giovanni [who]...made clothes for Mr. Jefferson and his servants". There was also "Antonine,...Francis, Madena and Belligrini, all gardiners". But what fascinated Isaac Jefferson most was his introduction to the Italian *cucina.* "The Italian people raised plenty of vegetables: cooked the most victuals of any people Isaac ever seen".[476]

Jefferson found the Italians to be congenial employees and model citizens of a republic. In fact, even before the farmers had moved from Colle to Monticello, Jefferson had written letters in which he had extolled their virtues. On June 8, 1778, Jefferson wrote to Giovanni Fabbroni a most curious letter, and it was especially curious that it was written while a war was going on. Jefferson told Fabbroni of his fondness for music and of his desire to form a band of musicians who could perform at Monticello. Noting that he had "among my domestic servants, a gardiner, a weaver, a cabinetmaker, and a stone-cutter to which I would add a Vigneron", Jefferson asked Fabbroni whether he, in a land where "music is much cultivated and practiced by every class of men", could find persons skilled in their trades and who could also be formed into a band of "two French horns, two clarinets and hautboys and a bassoon, without enlarging [my] domest[ic] expense". Jefferson suggested that should such persons be available, they might be contracted for a period of six years, after which they might choose to return to Tuscany or remain in America. Should Fabbroni be

drawing of the building in *Mazzei: My Life...,* following p. 202.

[476] "Life of Isaac Jefferson of Petersburg, Virginia, Blacksmith, Containing a full and faithful Account of Monticello and the Family there...". Slave memoir of Isaac Jefferson dictated to Charles Campbell in the 1840s, *WMQ,* Third Series, VIII (October, 1951), 569, 573, 581.

able to send the men, Jefferson would pay their passage from any French port.[477]

In fact, Jefferson was so pleased with his Italian neighbors that on August 30, 1778, he wrote to Richard Henry Lee, a Virginia representative in the Continental Congress:

> Emigrants [sic]...from the Meditteriane would be of much more value to our country in particular than from the more Northern countries. They bring with them a skill in agriculture and other arts better adapted to our climate. I believe that had our country been peopled thence we should now have been further advanced in rearing [sic] the several things our country is capable of producing.

Jefferson then uged Lee to use his influence in the Congress to approach Mazzei in "procuring emigrants".[478]

The Mazzei Italians did not remain at Monticello, for as Jefferson wrote in 1793, some of them had enlisted in the army, some took lands to work for themselves, and others found employment as gardeners by country gentlemen in the Virginia Piedmont.[479]

By that time, they were probably almost forgotten by Jefferson, then in Philadelphia as United States Secretary of State. Jefferson's observations, however, were superficially correct, but the careers of several of the Mazzei Italians can be traced with greater precision. Giovanni stayed on at Monticello for a while, and in 1780 he accompanied Madame Riedesel to New York. Anthony, too, remained at Monticello, but he was the unhappy one, wishing to return to Italy. Pellegrino spent some time in Philadelphia [480] and served briefly in the Continental Army.[481] Antonio Giannini, one of the men from Lucca, purchased a portion of Colle which he operated as a small farm.[482] Giannini's son, who spelled the name Gianniny, became a Baptist minister.[483] When Mazzei returned to Virginia in 1783, he found Vincenzo Rossi, his favorite, "living very comfortably with his wife and two small children". The older, who was six years of age, could read quite well, and the younger had just started going to school with his brother. Both were very well dressed. "So far as I could

[477] Thomas Jefferson to Giovanni Fabbroni, June 8, 1778, *Papers of Thomas Jefferson*, Boyd, ed., II, 196-197. Jefferson's Italian names for each craft (in parenthesis in the original) have been omitted.

[478] Thomas Jefferson to Richard Henry Lee, August 30, 1778, *VMHB*, VIII (July, 1900), 115-116.

[479] Thomas Jefferson to Albert Gallatin, June 25, 1793, in *The Writings of Thomas Jefferson*, Andrew A. Lipscomb, editor-in-chief, 20 volumes (Washington: The Thomas Jefferson Memorial Association, 1903), I, ix.

[480] Thomas Jefferson to Philip Mazzei, April 4, 1780, *Papers of Thomas Jefferson*, Boyd, ed. III, 342.

[481] A.F. Guidi, "Washington and the Italians", p. 34.

[482] P. Mazzei, *Memoirs*, p. 187.

[483] Edgar Wood, *Albemarle County in Virginia* (Charlotteville: Michie Company, 1901), p. 360.

learn", he wrote, "there was not one person from the original group that went over with me who had not bought some property".[484]

Mazzei's idyllic picture of the Rossi family stands in sharp contrast to his own American fortunes. Mazzei had hoped for a political career in the new republic, but he was never able to gain a political following. Despite his continued friendship with Jefferson, and despite Jefferson's efforts on his behalf, the failure of the Tuscan mission presented too much of an obstacle. Mazzei returned to Europe in 1785, never to return to Virginia. In 1791, that portion of Colle which had not already been disposed of in small tracts was sold for £250 to a Mr. Thomas.[485]

The Mazzei family story does not end here. When Mazzei went to Europe on his Tuscan mission, Mrs. Mazzei, who died soon thereafter, and Mazzei's step-daughter Maria Martini remained in Paris, where Mrs. Mazzei had relatives. There Maria met, and in 1780 married, Count Justin Pierre Plumard de Rieux, member of a family of the lesser nobility and a captain in the bodyguard of Louis XVI. The couple lived in Paris until 1783 when they sailed for America, landing in Charleston, South Carolina. In 1784, the de Rieux and their two small children went to Colle, but as the property was then being liquidated as a working farm, they moved to nearby Ash Lawn, where, for almost 12 years they farmed and operated a small school. In 1796 they moved to Goochland County and soon thereafter to Prince Edward County, where they again operated a school. When de Rieux died in 1824, Madame de Rieux moved to Richmond, where she died two years later and was buried in St. John's churchyard.[486]

Carlo Bellini was another Tuscan who came to Virginia the year after the arrival of Filippo Mazzei. Bellini was born in 1735, and although nothing is known of his formal education, it is assumed that he attended the University of Florence. Having been expelled (or exiled) from Tuscany for radical political ideas, he lived for a while in Paris, where he supported himself by giving lessons in Italian, then in London, where he made the acquaintance of Filippo Mazzei.[487]

It was probably through Mazzei's efforts that Bellini was allowed to return to his native land just at the time Mazzei was working out the final arrangements for his move to Virginia. Bellini, and again probably through Mazzei's good offices, received appointment to a minor position in the tax office of the Grand Duchy of Tuscany, but, again probably encouraged by Mazzei, Bellini, too, decided to go to Virginia.

Bellini was certainly not "brought" to Virginia as one of Mazzei's employees, and Mazzei, in fact, was somewhat surprised when Bellini and his wife arrived in

---

[484] P. Mazzei, *Memoirs*, p. 187.

[485] *VMHB*, LI (April, 1943), p. 119.

[486] Edwin R. Lancaster, "Books Read in Virginia in the Early 19th Century: 1806-1823", *VMHB*, XLVI (January, 1938), 59.

[487] Frank B. Evans, "Carlo Bellini and His Russian Friend, Fedor Karzhianin", *VMHB*, 88 (July, 1980), 339.

the colony in 1774. Mazzei did all that he could for the Bellinis, introducing them to the more prominent Virginia planters, taking them to Monticello to meet Thomas Jefferson, and putting them up at Colle for several years.[488]

The Bellinis were well received in Virginia. Some ten years after their arrival, Mrs. Bellini suffered an apoplectic stroke. Fearing that she was about to die, she told her husband, as Mazzei related the incident, "I don't want to die, because I don't feel that I have stayed long enough among these good folks".[489]

Like Mazzei, Bellini quickly became a Virginia citizen, and, as we have seen, had a brief and somewhat comical military career in the Albemarle Independent Company. Unlike Mazzei, however, Bellini espoused no particular causes, whether political or religious, and his emergence in the political scene was somewhat late.

In 1778, however, as the Virginia Council of State was receiving numerous letters from Europe written in French or Italian, Bellini was given what was intended as a minor appointment as Clerk of Foreign Correspondence to translate the documents. Bellini inflated the importance of the position by referring to himself in his European personal correspondence as "Secretary for Foreign Affairs".[490] Actually, the salary was 30,000 pounds of tobacco (the same as that of the Attorney General), compared with the Governor's 153,000 pounds.[491] This seems to have been the equivalent of £200 per annum,[492] and it enabled him to leave Colle and take up permanent residence in Williamsburg,[493] where he became active in the local Masonic Lodge.[494]

Also in 1778, and on the insistance of Thomas Jefferson, Bellini was appointed Professor of Modern Languages at the College of William and Mary, a position which he held for 24 years, thus becoming the first Italian academic in America and the first to teach Italian in an American college.[495]

There has been some question, however, as to Bellini's competence as a teacher, and from extant correspondence, we can find conflicting views. J. Sheldon Watson, a William and Mary undergraduate during the late 1790s, wrote to his brother that "Old Bellini professes to teach Modern Languages, which amounts to a total exclusion of the knowledge of them".[496] Jefferson, on the other hand, and perhaps in a better position to judge, found Bellini to be a

---

[488] *Ibid.*   [489] Mazzei, *Memoirs*, p. 200.

[490] Antonio Pace, Editorial note to a letter of Carlo Bellini to _____, August 12, 1778, in *WMQ*, Third Series, IV (July, 1947), 353n., 354n.

[491] *Papers of Thomas Jefferson*, Boyd ed., II, 274.

[492] Military Recommendations to the Governor and Council, May 15, 1778, *VMHB*, XXX (July, 1922), 288.

[493] F.B. Evans, "Carlo Bellini and His Russian Friend", p. 339.

[494] *Ibid.*, p. 342; *VMHB*, XXIX (April, 1921), 140n.

[495] A. DeConde, *Half Bitter, Half Sweet*, p. 5.

[496] J.S. Watson to David Watson, February 9, 1799, *VMHB*, XXIX (April, 1921), 140.

very fine teacher.[497] And yet, the same J. Sheldon Watson, shortly after graduation wrote:

> I have never [probably meaning "not"] yet seen Mr. Bellini. He is living now in an old house somewhere, I believe, near the [Governor's] Palace. The old fellow, as you suspect, is very poor; and to make his misfortunes greater, he has been almost deprived of the power of articulation by a paralytic attack. He has been for some time talking of removing his present lonesome habitation and fixing himself in [the] College. His only food, they say, is wine and biscuit; his only amusement — suffering.[498]

Bellini was, by this time, obviously infirm, and it was believed by some that he was totally unhappy, hoping to return to Tuscany to die, and being prevented therein only by lack of funds to pay for passage.[499] Although presented by one former student in a most pathetic fashion, another wrote in affectionate terms. In 1797, Carter Henry Harrison wrote to David Watson, who was about to visit Williamsburg:

> If you think it proper, you may make my best respects to the Bishop [Madison, President of the College of William and Mary], but that is just as you please — but certainly to Mr. Bellini.[500]

Even before the arrival in Virginia of Mazzei and Bellini, still another Italian of some distinction had put in his appearance. In 1772, the Scottsman, John Murray, Earl of Dunmore, came to Williamsburg as Virginia's last Royal Governor, and in his entourage was one Serafino Formicola, Lord Dunmore's *Maitre d'Hotel*, or steward. Formicola was a cultivated Neopolitan who had traveled extensively in Europe and who had once lived briefly in Russia.[501]

Formicola seems not to have been well acquainted with either Mazzei or Bellini during the early years of their life in Virginia, but this was probably because of Formicola's connections with the Royal Governor at a time when Mazzei was openly urging colonial revolt. In 1775, Lord Dunmore fled Virginia for England, and Formicola and his wife were left in Williamsburg totally without employment, although certainly not without friends.[502] Although he seems to have had no military experience during the Revolution, he is on the record as having been involved in small-scale military supply for the Virginia Militia.[503]

---

[497] *Ibid.,* 141n.

[498] J. Sheldon Watson to David Watson, November 4, 1799, *VMHB*, XXIX (April, 1921), 145.

[499] F.B. Evans, "Carlo Bellini and His Russian Friend", Pp. 346-347.

[500] Carter Henry Harrison to David Watson, June 11, 1797, *VMHB*, XXX (July, 1922), 228.

[501] G.E. Schiavo, *The Italians in America Before the Civil War*, p. 135.

[502] On May 25, 1775, Formicola was witness to the marriage of Thomas Skinner and Elizabeth Ryan. Abstracts of Marriage License Bonds on File in York County Clerk's Office, *WMQ*, First Series, I (July, 1892), 51.

[503] "Virginia State Troops in the Revolution, from State Auditor's Papers", *VMHB*, XXVII (July and October, 1919), 339.

When the Virginia capitol was moved from Williamsburg to Richmond in 1779, Formicola opened a tavern on the south side of Main Street, between 15th and 17th Streets. The structure was not a large one, having but two rooms on each of its two stories,[504] but the establishment soon became immensely popular. The Marquis de Chastelleux, one who was not given to praising American hostelries, visited Formicola's Tavern in 1781, noting both the proprietor's lavish hospitality and moderate charges.[505] Certainly this was worthy praise for what was a favorite gathering place for the Virginia gentry. One member of the Assembly, in settling an account for £6.6 in 1785, referred to the establishment as "my club at Formicola's", where "Generals, Colonels, Captains, Senators, Assemblymen, Judges, Doctors, and Clerks of every weight and calibre and every hue of dress, meet together at the fire, drinking, smoking, singing, and talking ribaldry".[506]

Despite his moderate charges, Formicola prospered and became, in fact, a man of considerable wealth. By the end of the Revolution, he owned seventeen slaves. He also became a man of influence in the little city which then had a population of a little more than 1,000. In April of 1782, he joined eight other businessmen petitioning the Virginia Assembly for leniency for James Hughes, a Richmond blacksmith, who has been convicted for treason. Whether it was the businessmen's petition or a rethinking of the need for Hughes's services to the town, the blacksmith was pardoned.[507] Formicola, although perhaps himself of no extensive formal education, had an interest in learning, having been one of the founders of the "Institute" in Richmond devoted to "the Sciences, Art, and Philosophy".[508]

Mrs. Formicola died on Monday, June 18, 1787, "after a short illness".[509] Perhaps Formicola thought that the tavern would not be a proper place of residence for a teenage girl (too much ribaldry?), and his daughter Eve was sent to live in Williamsburg, probably with the prominent Bankhead family.[510]

Eve became one of the leading belles of Williamsburg, and it would seem that she had been courted by most of the William and Mary undergraduates. Although she had given "encouragement" to several others, she finally married Stewart Bankhead.[511] Even before finally settling on Bankhead, Eve had

---

[504] Virginius Dabney, *Richmond: The Story of a City* (New York: Doubleday and Co., 1976), p. 36.

[505] G.E. Schiavo, *The Italians in America Before the Civil War*, p. 135.

[506] M.A. Musmanno, *The Story of the Italians in America*, p. 44n.

[507] H.M. Ward and H.E. Greer, Jr., *Richmond During the Revolution*, Pp. 147-148.

[508] *Tyler's Quarterly Historical and Genealogical Magazine*, II (January, 1921), 194.

[509] *Virginia Independent Chronicle*, June 20, 1787; *Virginia Gazette and Weekly Advertiser*, June 21, 1787.

[510] *Tyler's Quarterly*, II (January, 1921), 194. Formicola was listed in 1783 as owning a "lot" in Williamsburg. There was no mention of a house. *WMQ*, Second Series, XI (October, 1902), 114.

[511] Garrett Minor to David Watson, December 20, 1797, *VMHB*, XXX (July, 1922), 235, 235n.

prompted a letter from another former suitor. Garrett Minor who wrote in 1798 to his friend, David Watson:

> E. Formicola is moored irrevocably to Mr. Norfleet. On the whole, I admired Eve. She was fickle, inconstant, extravagant and coquettish. But she was endowed with sensibility and a share of sense which in some measure extenuated these qualities.

But Eve's coquettishness seems to have been totally forgiven, as Minor ended his letter of lament with a couplet from Alexander Pope:

> If to her some female Errors fall!
> Look on her face, and you'll forget them all.[512]

Eve Formicola's "Italian presence" was overwhelming!

---

[512] Garrett Minor to David Watson, April 28, 1798, *VMHB*, XXX (July, 1922), 245.

7

So What?

Philip Alexander Bruce once wrote, in his attempt to account for the non-English blood in Virginians' collective veins, that of the non-English who came to the colony,

> in nearly every instance [,] the person of foreign birth [and here we may certainly include English people of Italian extraction] intermarried with a Virginian, an English man or woman. Not only were his alien temper and sympathies thus moderated unnoticeably to himself, but the chance of his transmitting his own national traits to his offspring was thus lessened, if not destroyed. His descendants in the third generation, if not in the second, gave no indication whatever of foreign descent. The original foreign strains had in them at least been practically obliterated. They were so thoroughly English in feeling, moral standards, and general attitude of mind, as if no alien blood whatsoever coursed in their veins.[513]

A careful reading of Bruce's monumental pioneering work of Southern social history, *Social Life of Virginia in the Seventeenth Century,* will reveal, however, that the author had neither appreciation nor understanding of any of the non-English elements of Virginia society. As the documentation to the preceding chapters of the present study must make abundantly clear, Bruce was hardly aware of even an Italian presence, much less of an Italian influence.

Bruce was certainly correct in emphasizing the "Americanization" in Virginia of those of non-English origin, but in his application of the "melting pot idea" he was totally innocent of the biological facts of Virginia's European human origins, for even when he mentioned a name of a person of an origin other than one obviously from the British Isles, he was at something of a loss to provide an accurate identification.

Certainly the names of hundreds of persons of Italian origin on the foregoing pages, and even allowing for the exceedingly strong possibility (or probability) that some of the labelings are incorrect, there was, indeed, a strong infusion of Italian blood. To be sure, many of those identified as Italian were already of mixed blood, for even as Bruce found Virginians of non-English blood marrying those of English blood, the process had already begun in England. Using the

---

[513] Philp Alexander Bruce, *Social Life of Virginia in the Seventeenth Century* (Williamstown, Massachusetts: Corner House Publishers, reprint of 1968), Pp. 250-251.

Italian court musicians as examples, we find that there were few marriages within the families of the Musicians' Company, and that in the known cases (such as the Taliaferros, the Lupos and the Leneares), the "immigrant" was of one-fourth or one-eighth Italian blood. We have also seen that persons bearing common English names were also sometimes part Italian.

As to the degree to which seventeenth and eighteenth-century Virginians themselves were aware of an Italian presence, biologically or otherwise, it has already been pointed out that there was something of a "gravitation" of those of Italian origin to the Eastern Shore and to the lower counties on the south bank of the James River, and that the "presence" was reflected in such geographical (or cartographical) indications as the region "commonly called the Banks of Italy" and "Italia". At the risk of appearing to be facetious, one might ask whether there is any connection between the Italian ham known as prosciutto and the modern Smithfield ham which comes from that part of Virginia with these Italian cartographical identifications.

The fact is that of all the ethnic groups to find their way to Colonial Virginia (or even to Colonial America) the Italians have been the least conspicuous. This is due, in part, to their proportionally small numbers, and also, in part, to the rural nature of Virginia settlement, and, consequently, to the rural nature of Virginia society. Italian names were quickly anglicized, and we have seen numerous examples of these, but there is also the fact that since some persons of Italian origin had come to Virginia with the French, there was the assumption that these individuals were French, rather than Italian. It must be remembered, however, that just as there are "Englishmen of Italian extraction", there were also "Frenchmen of Italian extraction".

It is also apparent that Virginians of the colonial period were quite cosmopolitan in their attitudes toward the non-English. Seldom did the record indicate a national origin, and it may be assumed that there was no ethnic prejudice or condescention. From Edward Gargana in the first years of settlement to the arrival in the 1770s of Filippo Mazzei and his friends, Italians and others who came to the colony were accepted for their own worth — whether it was in the setting of a trading post for the Virginia Company or in propagandizing for the Revolutionary cause. A Virginian was simply, it would appear, a Virginian.

Although it would seem strange that a family such as the Taliaferros would not have been aware that their name might have seemed strange (in the spelling, if not in the pronunciation) in comparison with such "leading family" names as Cocke, Randolph, Lee, Jefferson, Carter, Grimes, or Byrd, it was not until the coming of Bellini and Mazzei that the Taliaferros were reminded of their Italian origin.

George Wythe, a Virginia signer of the Declaration of Independence and Professor of Law at the College of William and Mary, married, as his second wife, Elizabeth, the daughter of Richard and Eliza Taliaferro of James City County. Professor Carlo Bellini pointed out to Wythe that the name was, much to Wythe's surprise, Italian, even indicating the district and the village of Italy from which the name derived. Thomas Jefferson was then (1786) in Paris as Ambassador to the French court, and Wythe asked Jefferson to use his European contacts to try to provide a Taliaferro genealogy.[514]

Jefferson turned to Filippo Mazzei's old friend, Giovanni Fabbroni. Fabbroni set to work immediately, actually visiting two Tuscan villages where he interviewed the heads of several Taliaferro families. Fabbroni sent Jefferson the Taliaferro coat of arms and a genealogy as complete as he could construct it. The Tuscan Taliaferros were then, in sharp contrast to the large landholding Taliferros of Virginia, humble people, possessed of very small landholdings, and earning a living by "follow[ing] the straw hat trade".[515]

Fabbroni, however, erred, for on the basis of the information supplied by the Tuscan Taliaferros, he wrote that a member of the family "went to a strange country [presumably England] at the time of the great famine" in 1709.[516]

Obviously, Fabbroni was wrong, as the first Taliaferro (Robert) had come to Virginia in the 1640s.[517] Wythe, fully aware of Fabbroni's error, and certainly not pleased to learn that his wife's collateral line was of such lowly station, turned to genealogists in England, who provided him with various fanciful versions, locating Taliaferros in Scotland in 1500 and even with William the Conqueror in 1066.[518] It was not until 1969 that the Heralds College provided the definitive genealogy which traced Robert "the immigrant" to the Bartholomew who went from Venice to London in the days of Queen Elizabeth I.[519]

This somewhat belabored example might go a long way toward explaining that a "presence" does not necessarily indicate a "heritage". Nothing in the cultural life of the colony before 1773 in any way reflects the presence of several members of families of English court musicians, and nothing in the day-to-day life of either Virginia planters or small farmers, even to the slightest degree, suggests an Italian cultural influence. Even such geographical indications as "Italia" and "the Banks of Italy" merely suggest a concentration of persons bearing Italian names, not a community in any way culturally identified as "ethnic".

The "cultural" influence would have to wait until the arrival of Mazzei and his Italian friends, and the "influence" would then be a significant one and a direct one, and one coming from Tuscany without passing through an English way-station. By Mazzei's estimate, the Tuscan farmers introduced two score new

---

[514] William Buckner McGroarty, "The Taliaferro Family", *William and Mary Quarterly*, Second Series, IV (July, 1924), 191-192.

[515] Jean [Giovanni] Fabbroni to Thomas Jefferson, Florence, 20 July, 1786, *WMQ*, Second Series, IV (July, 1924), 192-194.

[516] *Ibid.*, p. 193.   [517] *See above.*

[518] W.B. McGroarty, "The Taliaferro Family", p. 195.

[519] *VMHB*, 77 (January, 1969), 22-25.

varieties of vegetables, vines, and trees, and Mazzei himself took credit for revolutionizing Virginia agriculture by his introducing winter wheat and fifty-day corn, known in Virginia as "Mazzei corn". Perhaps it might not be too fanciful to wonder whether the Tuscan tailor, Giovanni, might not have introduced a macaroni element into Virginians' masculine attire, as for several years he was kept busy making Tuscan hunting jackets for Jeffersons' friends and relatives.[520]

Through Carlo Bellini, the Italian language became something of a fad, if not an intellectual staple among those who attended the College of William and Mary. In Albemarle County spoken Italian became commonplace, as Thomas Jefferson practiced his Tuscan dialect with Mazzei's "peasants". Others, too, found the experience rewarding. On the gustatory level, Mazzei and others made their contribution, as both Mazzei and Thomas Adams, through their importing businesses, introduced Virginians to numerous items of diet apparently hitherto unknown in Virginia. As twentieth-century Americans are well aware, the Italian *cucina* is habit-forming — even to the point of addiction.

Virginia's eighteenth-century Italians probably did little to keep the colony clean and pure, and there is no evidence that they provided a lot of singers and judges (with the exception of the Taliaferros), but they did come through with a lot of "other swell people".

[520] P. Mazzei, *My Life...*, p. 204.

Index

Editor's Note: Please note that surnames are cited both individually, where a given name was available in the text, and collectively. Consequently, page citations for surnames represent the entire listing for that surname whether or not the individuals included are familially related. Variations of the surnames are also listed individually. Individual names which are identical, but which represent different persons are not repeated. As such, textual context must be consulted to determine personal identity.

5.00